T3-BOD-519

POPULAR FICTION 100 YEARS AGO

'Ah! my eyes grow dim,—my senses fail me,—my limbs refuse—oh!' and with a sigh she fainted in the arms of the deceiver.

Popular Fiction

100 years ago

AN UNEXPLORED TRACT OF
LITERARY HISTORY

Margaret Dalziel

PHILADELPHIA

DUFOUR EDITIONS

1958

© Margaret Dalziel 1957

First published in Great Britain by
Cohen & West Ltd   1957

PR
871
D3

40183

PRINTED IN GREAT BRITAIN

CONTENTS

ILLUSTRATIONS

*These illustrations from contemporary periodicals are repro-
duced by courtesy of the Trustees of the British Museum.*

INTRODUCTION

THERE arc few literary problems of such general interest as the dispute about comparative levels of taste at different periods of history. Laments about the 'common reader' occupy the professional critic or teacher; recollections of what their grandparents read sometimes trouble the subscribers of the threepenny and sixpenny lending libraries; an angry parent snatches the highly coloured comic from his offspring, with the remark that when he was young there wasn't all this trash putting ideas into kids' heads. The deterioration of taste (not of course always described in those words) is accepted by most people as an example of the natural tendency to degeneration shown everywhere in human life. There is much talk about the bad driving out the good, about 'mass-media', about the power of vested interests to force on the public books and periodicals produced with the sole object of making money. There is a general conviction that in literature as in life things are not what they used to be.

There is particular force in the conviction that 'popular' literature nowadays is far more degraded and degrading than that of earlier times. (By popular literature we understand here the books and magazines that are read purely for pleasure by people to whom pleasure is incompatible with the expenditure of intellectual or emotional effort.) It is widely believed that such modern publications as comics, crime fiction, and love stories of the 'true confession' type are much worse than their counterpart of former days. Yet an attempt to investigate the truth of this conviction brings one up against the fact that very little indeed is known about the popular literature of the past. The few modern writers who have touched on the subject deal with it briefly during the discussion of more considerable topics, or else confine themselves to a very small aspect of it.

The Victorians and their Books, by Amy Cruse, discusses books of every type and price, both fiction and non-fiction, and consequently devotes little space to the very cheap and often obscure novels and periodicals read by the people. E. E. Kellett's long discussion of the press in the second volume of *Early Victorian England* again concentrates on the more important newspapers and periodicals, though what he has to say about cheap journals is very just. Mr. and Mrs. Hammond in *The Age of the Chartists* have an excellent chapter on the beginnings of popular culture, but again they are dealing with literature only in a much wider context. *The Silver-fork School*, by M. W. Rosa, discusses the fashionable novel only; W. W. Watt's *Shilling Shockers of the Gothic School* is about one ephemeral though very interesting type of popular literature; while E. S. Turner's *Boys Will Be Boys* deals only with thrillers written chiefly for a juvenile public. Michael Sadleir's publications deal with novels rather than with periodicals, and are mainly bibliographical. J. M. S. Tompkins's excellent book, *The Popular Novel in England 1700-1800*, deals with novels at a time when they could be read only by a few comparatively wealthy people, and were therefore hardly popular in the widest sense of the term. And Q. D. Leavis's *Fiction and the Reading Public*, in its way a very stimulating discussion of popular literature, covers a wide field and, as far as the mid-nineteenth century is concerned, is undoubtedly somewhat misleading.

This book therefore has been written to show the reader what literature the great mass of the English people—the half or more of them who could read—could buy cheaply a hundred years ago. It was in the year 1841 that Edward Lloyd started to send from his publishing house in Salisbury Square large quantities of very cheap fiction, including the novels in penny parts to which the title 'penny dreadful' was first given. His success showed that there was a huge market for such literature, and he had innumerable followers. When it is added that in 1847 there began the first successful attempts at really cheap reprints of novels in volume form (as distinct from the novels published as serials in the early cheap periodicals, or in penny parts), it will be seen that the decade of the eighteen-forties brought about a literary revolution. For the first time in the history of England anyone could for the price of a penny buy up to sixteen large pages of reading matter, large pages of very small print, often illustrated into the bargain. It was a bargain that found plenty of takers.

Great quantities of this literature survive in British libraries. Quantities far too great for the patience of any modern reader. Volume after dusty volume can be lugged from the recesses where they have lain for a hundred years or more, *Family Heralds* and *London Journals* and their kind, each year's volume containing 832 big closely-printed pages, about two-thirds of which on the average consist of fiction. Hundreds and hundreds of 'yellowbacks', too, are to be found there—shilling reprints of successful two- and three-volume novels, originally sold at half a guinea a volume. And some of the original penny dreadfuls survive, through the lucky chance of having been bound in book form. Anyone interested in investigating the popular literature of the past is faced by a truly embarrassing plenitude of material, from which he is forced to select. Therefore the descriptions of these novels and periodicals in this book are acceptable only on the assumption that one quality of mass-produced fiction at any date is its great sameness. Most readers of modern magazines will, I think, accept this assumption, and certainly the reading of very large samples of the novels and magazines of a hundred years ago did nothing to contradict it.

Here then is presented some of the evidence needed for an informed comparison between popular literature today and that of the past. Perhaps it will make a small contribution towards more rational discussion of the question whether or not the people's literary taste has deteriorated during the last hundred years.

I

CHEAP LITERATURE BEFORE 1840

ALL popular literature is cheap in one sense of the term, and probably the major part of its definition is that it can be enjoyed with a minimum of effort on the part of the reader. The popularity of other kinds of entertainment, notably television and the cinema, is undoubtedly due in part to the fact that they share this quality. But the eighteen-forties saw the beginnings of a literature which was also cheap in the sense that it could be bought at a low price. At that time began the mass production of fiction which all but the poorest could afford to buy, of fiction therefore that was popular in the most fundamental way. Thus there emerged a phenomenon which has been worrying critics and moralists for over a hundred years, and which has a history both interesting and instructive. These years saw the large-scale production of penny periodicals and penny dreadfuls (the name given to novels published in penny weekly parts); and also the first systematic and successful attempts to issue full length novels at prices varying between one and two shillings. A whole new reading public came into being. The study of its tastes and demands is full of interest for the reader who is prepared to undertake it in a spirit of cheerful resignation to the fact that he is unlikely to discover lost treasures. What he will learn is what ordinary people a hundred years ago liked to read, and what kind of world their reading revealed to them.

The history of the Parlour and Railway Libraries, the two great series of cheap novels that appeared from 1847 and 1849 respectively, has already been told in some detail.[1] But not much is known of the steps by which it became possible for the very

[1] Michael Sadleir in *Collecting Yellowbacks*, 1938, and more recently in his *XIX Century Fiction*, 1951. See also his article, *Bentley's Standard Novel Series*, Edinburgh, 1932.

poorest to buy literature that set out to entertain rather than to reform or inform its readers. The readers of the Parlour and Railway Libraries certainly included members of the upper and uppermiddle classes, and few of the very poor, for even a shilling was too great a sum for the latter to spend on a book. But there were not so many who could not afford the penny which would buy a number of the *Family Herald*, or the *Mysteries of London*, or *Ada the Betrayed*, or the *Leisure Hour*, to name some very diverse successes in this line. So the history of cheap periodical publication in particular reflects the tastes and wishes of a huge public, and the way in which publishers and writers and moralists influenced and were influenced by it.

In a sense this history began in 1832, when three cheap weekly periodicals appeared for the first time, and by their immediate success showed the existence of a huge demand for cheap reading matter. But this demand was not something which grew up overnight. It is true that the invention of the steam printing press, which made its satisfaction possible, was fairly recent. But there is plenty of evidence to show that already the lower orders of Great Britain had their own literature.

For a long time they had been pretty well supplied with tracts. Both the Society for Promoting Christian Knowledge and the Religious Tract Society had been working for many years, while pious individuals often printed tracts at their own expense. Then for hundreds of years there had been chap-books—little books containing as a rule only one story, priced sometimes as low as a penny, though often as high as sixpence. These mostly related the adventures of worthies legendary and historical, Robin Hood, Jack the Giant-Killer, Jane Shore (there were many versions of her story), fair Rosamond, the blind beggar of Bethnal Green, and above all the Seven Champions of Christendom, about whom everybody seems to have read at some time or other. From time to time subjects were found among living people, so that there appear Mary, the Maid of the Inn (who discovered her lover to be a robber and a murderer) and Grace Darling. Another stock theme of the chap-books was popular superstition. They describe such things as the traditions associated with St. Agnes' and St. Valentine's Days, and different ways of telling fortunes and interpreting cards, and so on. Others contained poems, which varied between *Chevy Chase* and the *Royal Buffalo Songster*, or the *Real Virginny Melodist*. Often they had crude illustrations. But they were very small indeed, and the actual area of print (a real consideration with the type of reader for whom they were intended) was much less than that of the penny periodicals which were to appear in 1832.

At the very end of the eighteenth century had appeared 'bluebooks', which continued to be published till about 1820. A bluebook was an abridgement or imitation of a Gothic novel, usually of thirty-six or seventy-two pages stitched into a flimsy blue cover, and sold at sixpence or a shilling according to size. Typical titles were *Romano Castle, or, The Horrors of the Forest; The Mysterious Omen, or, Awful Retribution; The Black Forest, or, The Cavern of Horrors*. They tended to have for their settings a convent, monastery or Gothic castle, replete with the usual trappings of underground vaults, secret passages, animated portraits and mysterious manuscripts. Against this background moved the blameless hero and heroine, one or other frequently a foundling of unknown birth, the murderous villain, cruel parent, overbearing robbers, sorceresses, barons, monks, garrulous servants, peasants and banditti, all directly related to their prototypes in the full-length Gothic novel.

Then there were almanacs. Until 1836 these were subject to a heavy tax and were not very cheap, but from that year *Moore's Almanac* cost sixpence, and *Merlinus Liberatus*, another very old favourite, ninepence. These were full of vague prophecies about weather and political events. The more definitely astrological ones, like *Raphael's Prophetic Almanac*, gave horoscopes of famous persons and quite incomprehensible directions for casting a nativity. All of them contained lists of dates, tides, phases of the moon, and fragments of more or less useful information. Their circulation was considerable, and extends right up to modern times. So greatly was their influence deprecated (though they seem harmless enough to the modern reader) that one of the earliest publications of the Society for the Diffusion of Useful Knowledge was their *British Almanack*, which began in 1829. This, it was vainly hoped, would replace the others.

For many years there had been broadsides and single sheets giving accounts of crimes, last dying confessions of condemned criminals, and executions. A really good murder produced enough material for several separate sheets from one printer, and many different printers might write up a single case. Broadsides, like chap-books, were often printed in small provincial towns by the local printer. Trade in this kind of thing was still going on in 1851 when Mayhew was writing *London Labour and the London Poor*. There is a conventional style associated with them. They tend to open in some such manner as: 'It is with feelings of horror and regret that we have another murder to relate . . .', or: 'It is our painful task to record one of the most blood-thirsty murders committed in our County for Centuries. . . .' But their general tone is sober and decent enough, and certainly never worse than accounts of comparable events in modern newspapers.

And from the beginning of the century there had been many cheap periodicals advocating some political programme or other, frequently of a revolutionary kind. The work of Cobbett in this field is well known, but Cobbett is only the most celebrated of a whole tribe of republican, radical, reforming journalists whose little weekly papers, sold at a penny or perhaps twopence, flourished for a few months or years and then disappeared. There is no doubt that the support given to the Society for the Diffusion of Useful Knowledge, founded in 1825 to provide cheap informative literature with no political or religious bias, was largely due to a desire to combat radicalism. Nearly all these papers concentrated on opposition to the existing state of affairs, on putting forward a policy that was anti-Corn Law, anti-income tax, anti-Poor Law, anti-clerical, anti-Whig, anti-Tory, anti-Church and anti-Government. They were content for the most part to attack the world their readers knew rather than give them a Utopian vision of the world as it might be.

Tracts and chap-books, bluebooks and almanacs, broadsides and illegal newspapers of a radical tendency—all of these were reasonably cheap, and all of them circulated chiefly among the poor and the half-literate. Religion, romance, horror, crime,[1] astrology and revolution were the themes which had already shown themselves to have a strong popular appeal. But there was not enough literature at this level, and it was not yet cheap enough to circulate very widely.

The year 1832 changed all that. In that year appeared *Chambers' Edinburgh Journal*, the *Penny Magazine*, and the *Saturday Magazine;* each consisted of eight large pages every week; *Chambers' Journal* was the most expensive at a penny-halfpenny, the others cost a penny a number. The astonishment felt by the modern reader that such cheapness should be possible, having regard to the general price of books and newspapers at the time, can be no greater than that felt by readers in 1832. The success of the new publications was immediate. And their fortunes, considered in conjunction with their aims and methods, indicate very clearly what kind of cheap literature was shortly to become the most popular.

In 1825 had been founded the Society for the Diffusion of Useful Knowledge, supported by a large number of influential men, including Lord Brougham. Its object was to encourage the production of cheap literature which should be neither narrowly religious, entirely trivial, nor radical, revolutionary and atheistical. The *Penny Magazine*, which was published for them by Charles Knight, was almost at once immensely popular, a fact which did not endear it to papers like *The Times*, which pointed out with some bitterness that such cheapness was due to the fact that papers which carried no news were exempt from duty and taxation. They therefore had an unfair advantage over newspapers proper. Another reason for alarm was certainly the fear that, should the

---

[1] At this point it may be objected that no mention has been made of the *Newgate Calendar*, often referred to as if it were the daily reading of the British underworld during the later eighteenth and earlier nineteenth centuries. But the *Newgate Calendar* was expensive. For example, the famous edition of Knapp and Baldwin is listed in the *London Catalogue* of 1831 at two guineas for the five volumes.

stamp duty be repealed, Brougham would turn the *Penny Magazine* into a daily newspaper as a weapon in his war with *The Times*. But stamp duty was not repealed until 1855, and the *Penny Magazine* remained a weekly, austerely devoted to the dissemination of information. The first number promised that it would contain

> Striking points of Natural History—Accounts of the great works of Art in Sculpture and Painting—Descriptions of such Antiquities as possess historical interest—Personal Narratives of Travellers—Biographies of Men who have had a permanent influence on the condition of the world—Elementary Principles of Language and Numbers—Established facts in Statistics and Political Economy.

Derided by scholars like Dr. Arnold, who described it as 'all ramble-scramble', and by Tories like Barham, who believed that no good thing could come out of a society that had Lord Brougham as one of its leading members, the *Penny Magazine* for a time was unprecedentedly successful. By the end of 1832 it had a circulation, the publisher informs us, of 200,000. He was able to boast also that it had never contained

> a single sentence that could inflame a vicious appetite; and not a paragraph that could minister to prejudices and superstitions which a few years since were common. There have been no excitements for the lovers of the marvellous—no tattle or abuse for the gratification of a diseased taste for personality—and, above all, no party politics.

In that boast, alas, lay the cause of the decline and death of the *Penny Magazine*. So many of us have an incurable taste for the marvellous. As Knight himself wrote much later, when at the end of a long life he looked back with some complacency on his services to useful knowledge, the humbler classes did not find in his publications the aliment for which they hungered. They wanted fiction. And so in 1845 the *Penny Magazine* came to an end. The *Saturday Magazine*, published for the Society for the Promotion of Christian Knowledge as a counterblast to the secularism of the *Penny Magazine*, and equally dedicated to conveying solid information, lasted from 1832 till 1844. They were

2

by far the longest lived of a number of similar publications, among which should be mentioned *Leigh Hunt's London Journal*, begun in 1834 to express what Hunt in the opening number called 'the ornamental part of utility'. He offered for a very low price to introduce the poor to the pleasures of taste and scholarship, but this was not what they wanted either. Reading the few surviving copies of the *Halfpenny Magazines* and *Farthing Journals*, the *Penny Satirists* and *Penny Story Tellers*, which appeared during the years after 1832, only to vanish after the publication of a few numbers, one seems to see the publishers and writers exploring, however unsuccessfully, the potentialities of a new literary medium and the tastes of an unknown public.

The *Maids', Wives' and Widows' Magazine*, another cheap weekly which first appeared in 1832, was obviously significant for the development of cheap and popular literature, in which the magazine for women has been so important. This periodical was partly devoted to fashion, and contained illustrations and descriptions of clothes. The early numbers contained hints on domestic economy too, but these soon disappeared, leaving the field to fiction, poetry, 'extracts', and reviews of music, plays and literature. The intellectual standard is not high (typical of the comments on music is the following: 'Mr. Parry, Jun. is unquestionably the sweetest male ballad singer of the day'), but the character of the fiction in the early volumes is interesting. Some stories reflect an attitude of flippant cynicism, others overflow with early deaths and broken hearts and the whole paraphernalia of sensibility. Rouge is commended, but Sunday entertainments —'conversaziones'—condemned. This uneasy vacillation between the supposed standards of the fashionable world and the known prejudices of the evangelical lower and middle classes does not long continue, and in its later incarnation as the *Weekly Belle Assemblée* and the *New Monthly Belle Assemblée*, the *Maids', Wives' and Widows' Magazine* is almost wholly devoted to fiction and fashion. In this guise it survived till 1870, but it seems soon to have moved beyond the range of cheap to that of middle-priced periodicals.

One other publication of this early period should be mentioned, though it was not cheap, and did not, to use its own words, 'indulge in fictitious narrative'. The *Christian Lady's Magazine* is important both as reflecting the views of a numerous and very influential section of the English people at that time, the extreme evangelicals, and as being to some extent the prototype of many later publications, some of which *were* cheap. At this date, however, its message was proclaimed at the working-class level by tracts, written in a tradition that went back to the eighteenth century. When a new tradition of communicating with the lower orders was established, that of the cheap weekly periodical containing a certain proportion of fiction, various religious organizations adapted it to their own purposes. The relentlessly evangelical message of the *Christian Lady's Magazine* is later taken up by the *Churchman's Monthly Penny Magazine* from 1846, the *Leisure Hour* from 1852, the *Sunday at Home* from 1854, and the *Family Treasury of Sunday Reading* from 1859. These were at the price and in the form which was gradually being developed during the eighteen-thirties and forties.

It is significant that the one steadily and permanently successful cheap periodical to begin at this period (it ceased to exist only a year ago) was begun by a business man. William Chambers had a much better idea than Charles Knight of what his readers would find interesting. Child of the age which found in the dissemination of useful knowledge a finer ideal than the promotion of Christian knowledge, he wrote in an early number of his *Journal* as follows:

> Mr. Chambers would be happy, for his own part, to make the work exclusively of a useful cast, but he fears that what might be added to its solidity would detract from its circulation, and, consequently, lessen its real usefulness. He conceives that so long as good taste is not offended, the frivolous matters of lighter literature serve the same good end as the wings attached to certain seeds, by which they are carried away and diffused over the earth.

The *Journal* would of course contain many articles of an informative kind, and in the very first number he expressed his wish 'to take advantage of the universal appetite for instruction which at present exists; to supply to that appetite food of the best kind, and in such a form, and at such a price, as must suit the convenience of *every man in the British dominions'*. On the other hand, he had every intention of getting as high a circulation as he could, and from the first *Chambers' Journal* included sketches and stories, generally sober and realistic but unmistakably fictitious. This single-minded concentration on the essential matter of circulation was going to be very important in the development of cheap fiction, and it is interesting to see it openly displayed at this early date. Consciously or unconsciously, Chambers recognized that as reading became more and more an everyday accomplishment, so there grew up an increasing proportion of readers who regarded it as a means of entertainment rather than of instruction. These were not people who had toiled to learn to read in order to have access to the wisdom of the ages—or even in order to qualify for a better job. Despite the very imperfect organization of education at this date, many lower-class people were already having literacy thrust upon them. Many of them lived lives of unspeakable degradation, most of them could hope for nothing better than a drab existence enlivened by few pleasures and fewer hopes. What they wanted was not cheap knowledge but cheap amusement, not information but fiction. This want was supplied, not by philanthropic societies, but by business men.

II

SALISBURY SQUARE FICTION

CHAMBERS, like any other business man, wanted to make money. But he was also genuinely interested in providing good reading at a price the poor man could pay. Yet though his *Journal* showed how cheaply and profitably such a periodical could be produced, its real appeal was to the lower-middle rather than the lower classes. Its tone was sober, respectable, bourgeois—a scurrilous paper called the *People's Police Gazette* in 1841 described Chambers as having prostituted himself to the full-fed and crop-sick corn monopolists and to the bloated mill-owning proprietors of the factory slaves. It was another business man, Edward Lloyd, who judged the taste of the poorest readers more accurately than Chambers had. For about ten years, beginning in 1841, Lloyd published a number of cheap periodicals and a long list of novels appearing in penny weekly parts; it was these latter to which the title 'penny dreadful' was first given. From his address in Salisbury Square was derived the name 'Salisbury Square Fiction' by which such stories soon began to be known.

There is no doubt that Lloyd published both the penny dreadfuls and the penny periodicals (such as his *Penny Sunday Times and People's Police Gazette*, his *Penny Weekly Miscellany*, and the *People's Periodical and Family Library*, to name only some of them) to make money. In 1842 he established a newspaper, which under the title *Lloyd's Weekly Newspaper* ran till 1918 and was finally incorporated in the *Sunday Graphic* in 1931. This was his main interest, and as it became self-supporting he gradually stopped publishing penny fiction. Later in life, we are told, he much disliked being reminded of these early ventures. But at the time he expressed in unctuous phrases his pleasure and pride in being able to provide wholesome entertainment for the industrious classes. The following extract from the preface to the first complete volume of his *Penny Weekly Miscellany*, is a good example of his oily sentiments and florid style:

> We must likewise, in some degree, claim for ourselves the merit, if we may be allowed the term, of laying before a large and intelligent class of readers, at a charge comparatively insignificant, those same pleasures of the imagination which have hitherto, to a great extent, only graced the polished leisure of the wealthy; and, at the same time that we have done so, we have found with unmingled satisfaction that correct tastes, glowing fancies, and an admirable perception of the poetical and the beautiful, are as well to be found by the humblest fire-sides, as in the lordly mansions of the great and the noble.

The nature of these pleasures of the imagination to which so many readers were being introduced for the first time is best indicated by an example. One of the most prolific writers published by Lloyd was Thomas Peckett Prest. Typical both of Prest's novels and of penny dreadfuls in general (whether they appeared as serials in the weeklies, or in penny parts) is one called *Vice and its Victim; or, Phoebe, the Peasant's Daughter*. The lovely Phoebe Mayfield, described in the text as a 'too confiding, simple village maiden', is the daughter of an aged and worthy couple. The profligate Lord Selborne wins her heart, overcomes her scruples, and, promising marriage, persuades her to elope with him (despite the very discouraging utterances of a mysterious 'gipsy sybil', who warns Phoebe that no good can come of this course of action).

The most immediate result is that on discovering what her daughter has done Mrs. Mayfield dies of shock, while Mr. Mayfield presently becomes insane.

Meanwhile, the trusting Phoebe is 'married' to Lord Selborne, and is leading a pretty enjoyable existence when she learns her true position. She therefore runs away, and returns to her native village and to the care of her faithful lover, Henry Ashford, his sister Amy, and various other kind friends. Henry is taken up by a press gang and goes to sea, where he has many adventures, and encounters both Lord Selborne, now deeply repentant for his treatment of Phoebe, and his friend Captain Beaufort, who has taken to a life of crime.

Phoebe and her friends tend her father, whose madness persists; his ravings about his faithless daughter cause her a great deal of anguish. Eventually Henry returns from sea, and, inheriting some property, settles down as a country gentleman. Phoebe and he are affianced, but their nuptials are delayed.

Captain Beaufort has now become a confirmed criminal, though he suffers from bad bouts of remorse. Led by a low character called Sam Filcher, he engages in robbery and occasional murder, and their tediously repetitive exploits fill many pages. Among other crimes, they set fire to Henry Ashford's house and barns, and rob and murder Lord Selborne. But this is all for the best, as Beaufort has long known that Phoebe's marriage was perfectly legal. When this secret is revealed, on the last page but one, Mr. Mayfield, newly restored to his senses, cries: 'Oh, thank heaven, then I can again wi'out a blush o' sheeame, press thee to my throbbing heart an' call thee daughter'. Phoebe and Henry Ashford marry and live happily ever after, while Beaufort and Sam Filcher are captured and hanged on the last page of all.

This story shows the double intention of most such literature. It is not enough just to shock and startle by accounts of horror and crime. Such modern writers as confine themselves to this one aim must at least relieve the monotony of their accounts of violence by directing the reader's attention to sexual aberration or to the love life of criminal or detective. The older way to hold the reader's attention, and one that is morally less objectionable, is to arouse his sympathy for the good character, especially the heroine. That this was an essential part of the early penny dreadfuls is not often realized. Many of us are familiar with the lurid events of one or two classics like the story of Sweeny Todd. We commonly think of penny dreadfuls as exclusively devoted to the description of the exploits of highwaymen and notorious criminals. And it is true that from the sixties onward penny dreadfuls were directed towards a juvenile public (of course it included many adults, just as the readers of comics today do) and dealt only in blood and thunder. But the early stories were far from being simple tales of terror, violence and crime. As in the Gothic novel, sensibility and sensation were of equal importance. The heroine's feelings were as prominent as the murders, duels, family feuds, robberies, love potions, father's curses, ghosts, poison and revenge by which she was surrounded. Often, as in *Vice and its Victim*, the two elements in the plot are hardly connected at all. Phoebe, her faithful lover, aristocratic seducer and heart-broken father belong to the world of highly coloured romance; the other characters belong to a kind of gangster fiction, of which we regard the *Newgate Calendar* as the prototype, dealing only with the plotting, execution and punishment of actual crime. Phoebe is not even abducted by the criminals, one very common way of involving the two sets of characters with each other.

The stories in themselves afflict the modern reader with immense boredom, varied only by occasional delight at some particularly marked absurdity. They constantly repeat stock situations and characters, such as the English setting (in contrast with stories in the expensive magazines, which preserved the Gothic tradition of an alien aristocracy as the actors in sensational literature, the tradition of the Italian count, the German princeling, the Spanish brigand of concealed but lofty lineage); the comparatively lowly social position of the heroine (who nevertheless speaks standard English, though her parents speak an unidentifiable *patois*); the nautical hero; the foundling motif; the abduction of the heroine; the seduction of an innocent girl by a designing aristocrat; the use of the supernatural, with prophecies and premonitions (often connected with gipsies); strong domestic affection; the purely passive role of the heroine (Phoebe faints twenty-eight times in the course of the story); the power of the emotions, particularly grief and remorse, which frequently cause illness, madness or death; the restrained attitude to sex; and the triumph of virtue over vice. The rigid observance of these conventions is one cause of the overwhelming sameness of these stories.

Another reason for their tedium is the trick of repeating the same episodes over and over again in one story. In *Vice and its Victim* occur several almost identical accounts of conversations in which Lord Selborne tries to persuade Phoebe to elope with him, of scenes between Phoebe and her mad father, of scenes in which he or she weeps over the grave of her mother, and of scenes in which the two criminals plan a robbery, execute it, are almost captured, escape and, caught in a storm, finally reach a safe place and settle down to a carouse to celebrate their success. Only in this way can a very meagre plot be stretched out to cover 574 octavo pages, in double columns of very small print. This trick is regularly used in both serials and penny dreadfuls at this time.

There is nothing about the delineation of character in these stories to make them better reading. The virtues of the hero and heroine are as tedious as the unredeemed iniquity of the villains, and the rustic lover and his lass, frequently introduced for comic effect, are worse than all. As is natural with literature produced so fast, so copiously and so cheaply, the process of stereotyping character, as well as incident, is carried as far as possible.

The other most important quality of this fiction is its style. There are numerous and often funny mistakes in grammar, like 'Scalvoni strided in', 'Hubert, thou has destroyed me', or, passing for a complete sentence: 'Blanche, as I have before stated, was young and beautiful but whose impetuosity of temper was her only fault'—all taken from *Lloyd's Penny Weekly Miscellany*. There are well mixed metaphors, like 'If at times a relic of the past came over him, he brushed it away from his mind', and such gems as 'I had forsaken her, for I had got palled'. But apart from grammatical mistakes the style has a character all its own. Even if there were no external evidence of the connection between early penny dreadfuls and serials on the one hand and the popular melodrama on the other, the signs of dramatic technique in the stories would lead one to suspect it. Soliloquy, rhetorical question, exclamation, aposiopesis and apostrophe abound, used more freely in Prest's books than in the serials but never absent. The use of the second person singular is common, and frequently incorrect. Events and scenes which in a novel are mostly described by the writer are made part of the dialogue, as is often necessary in a play. The language generally is highly figurative, full of cliché and platitude, and extremely ornate. (In this respect it is interestingly like much of the poorer and more pretentious popular literature today.) There is little attempt to reproduce the natural forms of speech, and one of the most genuinely amusing things about some of the stories is the stilted and ladylike phraseology of the criminal characters.

When, in *Vice and its Victim*, Henry Ashford leaves his Phoebe, it is with the following words:

> 'Courage, Phoebe, courage, trust in that sweet little cherub who sits up aloft, and will ever keep watch for the safety of the hardy mariner while tossed about on the angry billows, or exposed to the cannon balls of the enemies for that sea-girt isle, the proud land of his birth.'

Another lover, in *Ernestine de Lacy; or, the Robber's Foundling*, also by Prest, leaves his lady with these words:

> 'I go from hence; and while life's purple current still flows within my veins, although another shall possess thine heart, thine hand, my constant prayers shall be offered up to Heaven for thine happiness.'

On a single page of *Lloyd's Penny Weekly Miscellany*, chosen at random, appear these phrases: 'Tempt me not to touch the polluted gold'; 'The iron has indeed entered my soul'; 'For many weeks she lay hovering 'twixt life and death'; 'The common necessaries of existence'; 'Go in peace'; 'a voice nearly inarticulate from deep emotion'; and 'Are you his wife?' 'In all but the name, father.' In *The Maniac Father*, Rosabelle's grief is thus described:

> Sobs heaved her bosom, and tears alternately chased each other down the poor persecuted one's pale cheeks; and it was very evident that she felt more than usually depressed even than she had done for some time, even under all the many afflicting circumstances under which she had been so frequently placed.

And when she left her seducer, he reacted in a very typical way:

> 'Gone!' gasped forth Beresford, in a tone of agony, starting, and striking his forehead; 'Rosabelle gone! through storm and tempest; fled from me! Great God! should she—ah! What but deepest guilt could nurture such foreboding? Should consciousness of shame and misery have led her to despair; should my fell treachery have—bah!

Rosabelle a suicide—I am a MURDERER! a double murder! Traitor to love and nature! Outcast of Heaven and man! Seducer, destroyer, a perjured lover, and a blood-stained father! Oh, villain! damned villain! Rosabelle! Rosabelle! I knew not half thy value till thy loss!'

While the short stories in Lloyd's periodicals tended to be less exciting than the serials and penny dreadfuls, they had a sensationalism of their own. A typical story was entitled *Count Florine; or, Treachery Baffled*. It opens as follows:

The faint rays of the departing sun were smiling pleasantly upon the small country town of S——, and the full moon of a summer's eve was bursting forth from the tricoloured clouds of the ethereal canopy. The wearied traveller was judiciously seeking his nearest resting-place; and the hard-working, though comely labourer, was returning from the fatigues of the day, to cheer once more his welcome hearth, and thrice-welcome his family.

This idyll is interrupted by the machinations of the villain, who brings to the heroine false news of her lover's death. She behaves as a heroine should:

She shuddered, wept, and laughed.
But was the latter natural? No; it was that wild and hollow laugh which generally attends the paroxysm of despair and disappointment; presently her now rayless eyes rolled within their orbits, and her whole frame shook convulsively. She reeled, and fell fortunately into the outstretched arms of Sir Henry Maurice.

After weeks and weeks of brain fever she recovers and is on the point of making a reluctant match with the villain—is at the very altar—when her true love returns, treachery is unmasked, and her happiness restored. This kind of story was much more like those in the expensive magazines designed for women than were the full-length novels. It is also closer to the Gothic novel, as for, example, in the introductory passage, with its description of nightfall, in the nationality and social position of the characters, and in the absence of lower-class villainy, the highway robbery, smuggling, thieving or body-snatching of the full-length penny dreadful. And it foreshadowed the next stage in the development of penny fiction.

But in the meantime stories like *Vice and its Victim* were de-voured by the new reading public. There could no longer be any doubt that there was a strong demand for cheap fiction of this kind. This was what the poor needed, escape into a world of exciting activity, of vice and crime, of love and suffering. The semi-literate pored over the vile blurred print, the illiterate gaped at the stiffly unrealistic illustrations and bribed the literate to read the stories aloud to them, while the middle classes complained of the moral, or rather immoral influence of such reading matter. Lloyd added volume after volume to his list, using every adver-tising device known to the time (including paying half his men's wages in copper coin stamped with his own advertisements, till this was made illegal). Every detail of his business had his personal attention. Sala, working as a young man for the wood-engraver who was supplying Lloyd with the blocks for illustrating the penny dreadfuls, received a letter from the publisher: 'The eyes', he wrote, 'must be larger, and there must be more blood—much more blood!' More and more writers turned their attention to such stories, mere children were, some said, paid starvation wages to do the composing, and the steam presses groaned and shuddered in their efforts to keep pace with yet another demand revealed or created by the industrial revolution, the demand for mass-pro-duced literature for the masses.

III

WEEKLY ROMANCE

WHILE Lloyd with his penny dreadfuls had the first outstanding success in the publication of cheap fiction, it did not last long. In *London Labour and the London Poor*, the first volumes of which appeared in 1851, Mayhew ends his section on the literature of the costermongers by saying:

> The tales of robbery and bloodshed, of heroic, eloquent, and gentlemanly highwaymen, or of gipsies turning out to be nobles, now interest the costermongers but little, although they found great delight in such stories a few years back. Works relating to Courts, potentates, or 'haristocrats', are the most relished by these rude people.

Though this needs to be qualified, for the most popular periodicals continued to flog the foundling theme long after this, it is true that the taste for reading about 'haristocrats', or at least about members of the middle as opposed to those of the lower classes, soon began to assert itself. In some of the short stories in his penny weeklies Lloyd himself had catered for it. In the serials and penny dreadfuls most of the characters, including the hero and heroine, were of humble origin. Excitement was provided by low crimes like robbery, thieving, smuggling and body-snatching, and members of the upper classes, who appeared from time to time as either heroes or villains, were in the minority. But most of the short stories were about members of the middle and upper classes. In these sentiment began to prevail over sensation, and the sensation to change its character. Villainy abounded, but it was high-bred villainy, relating to things like the inheritance of property, the succession to titles, and the ruining of rivals in business and love. These stories were frequently set in foreign countries, and were recognizably similar to those that were appearing in the expensive magazines which would never have

printed anything like the penny dreadfuls. If Lloyd had been
interested in continuing to publish cheap fiction, his chances of
success would have depended on his readiness to change over from
penny dreadfuls to serials with this different appeal. That this was
the kind of thing the public was coming to prefer is shown by the
outstanding success of three penny weeklies established between
1843 and 1846, all of which went in very largely for stories of
'haristocrats'. These were the *Family Herald*, the *London Journal*
and *Reynolds's Weekly Miscellany*. With their establishment a new
era in the publication of cheap fiction had begun.

The amount of information that can be discovered about these
periodicals is a sign that the new industry was beginning to be
organized. The early history of the *London Journal*, for example,
which ran from 1845 till 1912, is the history of a successful
business venture. It began as the speculation of a man called
George Stiff, an engraver who had been dismissed from the staff
of the *Illustrated London News* for incompetence. Once the publication was launched, he managed to get sufficiently into debt to
the firm who supplied him with paper for them to keep him on
his feet till he was established. The first editor was G. W. M.
Reynolds, later a prominent Chartist, who left in 1846 to found
his own *Miscellany*, a publication of the same type. Already the
commercial possibilities must have been apparent. Reynolds's
place was taken by J. F. Smith, whose immensely long and popular
serials were the chief factor in the success of the *London Journal*.
Circulation would rise by as much as 50,000 as one of his stories
drew to its close. Later Cassell enticed Smith away from the
London Journal and on to the staff of his *Illustrated Family Paper*,
but Stiff, who seems to have had a flair for getting hold of the
right man, replaced him by Pierce Egan the younger.

In 1858 Stiff sold the *Journal* to Ingram and McMurray for
£24,000—a pretty considerable fortune. At first the new proprietors tried to alter the tone of the fiction, and serialized *Kenil-
worth* and *The Fortunes of Nigel*. But there was always a serial of
Egan's running at the same time, and from 1860 Scott was
quietly dropped, while Egan remained a regular contributor till

his death in 1880. He died, Sala tells us, 'a prosperous gentleman'.

This story has been told at some length because it is an instructive one. Several people are here shown to have made a very good thing out of cheap fiction. And the increasing prominence and establishment of the industry are shown in other ways. Circulation figures for such periodicals were sometimes known, and are quoted by reputable writers like Charles Knight, Wilkie Collins and Henry Vizetelly. Their form was becoming standardized. Sixteen pages in each number was the rule, and very few of the new periodicals that were continually starting up departed from it. Soon it became the custom to offer for sale bound volumes containing a year's numbers. And, most important of all, an effort was made by printing all sorts of things other than fiction to attract the reader who would not have touched a penny dreadful proper with a pair of tongs, but who found the relentlessly informative pages of the *Penny Magazine* rather heavy going, and longed for romance. What periodicals like the *London Journal* and the *Family Herald* did was to combine the merits and avoid the defects of such really cheap publications as had so far appeared. Avoiding the sober realism of *Chambers' Journal* and the *Penny Magazine*, they yet attained a certain degree of respectability; avoiding the sordid realism of Salisbury Square fiction, they achieved an equal degree of excitement. In addition to romantic stories, they printed recipes, handy hints, short informative articles and letters from correspondents. They therefore attracted a very much larger reading public than their predecessors. In 1854 Charles Knight estimated the circulation of the *Family Herald*, the *London Journal*, and *Reynolds's Miscellany* as 300,000, 450,000 and 200,000 respectively,[1] and in 1858 Wilkie Collins accepted as very likely the claim of the most popular penny weekly (almost certainly the *London Journal*) to a circulation of half a million.[2] Here obviously is a new and profitable industry well under way.

[1] Alice A. Clowes, *Charles Knight*, 1892, p. 226.
[2] *Household Words*, xviii (August 21, 1858), 221. Reprinted in *My Miscellanies*, 1863.

The very name of the first of these periodicals to establish itself,
the *Family Herald*, was at once an inspiration and an augury. It
was calculated to inspire confidence in the most censorious breast,
and it was the forerunner of a host of more or less similar publications in whose titles the words 'family', 'home', 'domestic',
'household' and the like indicated their claim to respectability.
The first number of the *Family Herald* states the policy that is to
be followed:

> The prejudice against cheap publications will probably disappear
> when it is made apparent that the 'FAMILY HERALD' will be conducted
> in accordance with its motto, 'INTERESTING TO ALL—OFFENSIVE TO
> NONE'—without reference to party feeling or religious predilections,
> being neither the advocate of any popular theory, nor the apologist
> for delusive schemes.

There will be sedulous avoidance of anything

> tending to inflame, excite, or even disturb the mind of man in the
> performance of his imperative duties—no controversial doctrine will
> occupy the space destined for instructive fictions or authenticated
> facts.

'Pleasing and harmless recreation for all the members of a family'
is promised, for, England having become 'a reading and thinking
nation', cheap, useful and innoxious reading must be provided,
something

> a step above those dull and moody publications which are not read
> though given as a present, or those which are greedily bought up,
> because they inflame the imagination, flatter the passions, corrupt
> the morals, and lull to sleep the mental energies.

This moral claim is again put forward over a year later, when
an editorial entitled 'The Penny Press; Its Probable Destiny' makes
the general assertion that penny papers are in this respect superior
to the monthlies and to the daily papers. In fact, they

> will not yield to the quarterlies themselves in . . . respect for the
> domestic virtues . . . there is no penny paper extant which professedly
> deals in obscenity or private slander. The people is a moral censor,
> and publicity is the guarantee of decorum. Certain advertisements,
> even of the morning and evening papers, would destroy the circula-
> tion of any penny paper in London.

Certainly, whatever one's opinion of the assumptions and implications of its fiction, the contents of the *Family Herald* are respectable. They included in the early years an editorial each week, articles and sketches of a general kind dealing with travel, biography, simple science, current topics and events, poetry, notes on fashions and gardening, book reviews (mostly made up of long extracts), snippets of all sorts, recipes from how to make a rich plum pudding to how to get rid of bed bugs, and finally the answers to correspondents which were to become one of its most famous features. Contributors to the first volume include such unexceptionable writers as Mrs. Norton, Mary Howitt and Eliza Cook. The articles and sketches are very similar in subject matter to those in the *Penny Magazine*, for example, though shorter as a rule and less thorough; except that no bones are made about ventilating some of the more generally discussed social problems of the day. The *Penny Magazine* had not concerned itself with governesses, or health of towns, or attacked the complicated system of local government which made sanitary reform so difficult, but the *Family Herald* rushed in, even forgetting its usual anti-partisan attitude at times in a spirited attack on the rich.

The tone of the editorials is from the beginning curious. It is lofty, expressing strong anti-clerical and anti-sectarian feeling, but a diffused sort of Christianity instead. This was to be very important in determining the attitude taken up towards such periodicals by the evangelicals. Instead of orthodox religious ideas we find at times a cautious republicanism and vague philosophical speculation. The sentiments expressed were not as a rule such as to appeal to the vigorously pious, and woolly reasoning often makes them exasperating to the modern reader, but they were harmless enough. The poetry, like most of what appears in such publications, is worth special study. The answers to correspondents are on the whole serious and sensible, resisting the temptation to scoffing and flippancy offered by the nature of many of the questions.

One lady asks how and on what terms she may be admitted to a nunnery—she is referred to a priest. 'A Servant Lassie', who has

3

written that next to her Bible and the *Family Herald* she derives the greatest pleasure from reading Shakespeare, Byron, Pope, or any other book she can lay hands on, is told that 'if she can make herself happier and wiser by reading it is her duty to do so'. But the editor must point out that one of the best servants he knows cannot read or write, so that all her learning is professional, 'and her memory is filled with ideas belonging to her station'. 'Elizabeth P.' has allowed her lover 'to anticipate the marriage day', and though she has escaped exposure she is deeply unhappy. She is told that while virtue is irrecoverable, and she can never be truly happy again, yet there are other resources open to her; 'but if you merely regret the past without accepting it, you will be miserable to no purpose'. An answer to an enquiry concerning Sunday travel is moderate but disapproving: 'Habitual Sunday strollers are, with very few exceptions, persons of loose principles, scoffers at sacred subjects, and mere sensualists.' Within the limitations of their day and time these answers are all fair enough, and we find some, like that addressed to 'Elizabeth P.', which show excellent sense. On theology, which comes next to affairs of the heart as a subject for readers' queries, we find more pretension and less certainty, as when an enquiry about Unitarianism evokes the reply that Unitarianism is necessary in the church to correct the excesses of Trinitarians, but that it makes the error of 'denying the divinity of humanity—a magnificent doctrine, which may be modified, but never abandoned'. It is hard to see such an answer being very helpful to readers of the *Family Herald*.

As time passed, and other similar periodicals began to compete with the *Family Herald*, we find an increase in the proportion of fiction. This was to be a general trend in these works. In addition, the rest of the contents became less serious. Connected articles giving useful information were replaced by snippets. Jokes, riddles, 'varieties', the editorial and answers to correspondents were by 1855 the modicum of ballast that had to give weight to a great deal of story-telling.

A serial published in the *Family Herald* in 1844, entitled *Julia Tremaine; or, a Father's Wish and a Husband's Duty* will give a good

idea of the sort of story that from 1843 onwards was being
produced in huge quantities in these penny periodicals.

> Lord de Moreton (we are told) was descended from ancient and
> honourable ancestors, and pride, his lordship's ruling passion, was
> an hereditary feeling; for it was his boast that plebian blood had
> never flown in the veins of anyone who had borne the title of
> Moreton.

Lady de Moreton had died young, for

> the hectic flush on the cheek of Julia too plainly bespoke consump-
> tion, whilst the dazzling lustre of her beautiful eyes pronounced too
> fatally that she was gradually sinking, an early victim to the grave.

Left to bring up his orphan children alone, Lord de Moreton plans
the union of his son, Harcourt Lord Tremaine, with his lovely
cousin, the Lady Julia Newbourg, the young people consenting.

But while at Oxford Lord Tremaine is enmeshed in the toils of
Lady Maria Priam, sister of Lord Ashton, 'a fellow collegian'.
Lady Maria is a designing hussy who at the bare suggestion of his
departure for home and Julia has 'recourse to tears and an hysteric'.
But Lord de Moreton swoops down and carries his son home,
where the attractions of Lady Julia soon reconcile Lord Tremaine
to his lot. The first sight of her is enough:

> She was dressed in pale blue gauze, the sleeves composed of deep
> blond, which added lightness to her sylph-like figure; her fine dark
> hair fell in long and graceful ringlets on a neck and shoulders whose
> whiteness would have vied with marble.

They are married amid scenes of great splendour, and all promises
well.

However, they go to London for the season, and there Maria
is lying in wait, brooding over her wrongs. She writes to the
bridegroom:

> 'If Lord Tremaine has not lost all feeling, he will, the first oppor-
> tunity he can detach himself from the idol of his affections, call in
> Bruton Street, where he will behold the victim his cruelty has made
> in the unfortunate MARIA.'

The rest of the story is a chronicle of the sufferings nobly borne
by Julia, and the struggles of her husband to free himself from

Maria's clutches. We are told of Julia that many a night she 'watered her pillow with the bitter tears of affliction'; yet, throughout trials which include being left alone with servants in a foreign country, both while she has her first baby, and later when it dies, she is seldom even tempted to be other than patient— though at one stage she so far forgot herself that 'resentment had some share in her feelings, and, for a moment, she wronged her pure and gentle nature by supposing herself capable of reproaching him for his perfidy'. But of course she doesn't, and her spirit is shown only when Maria's brother makes dishonourable proposals to her, threatening that unless she flees with him his vengeance will fall on Lord Tremaine, as the seducer of his sister.

'Wretch!' exclaimed Julia, her countenance lighted up with contempt. 'Wretch! Too insignificant for my anger! Know that I despise your threats equally with your promises! And did I but possess the means of acquainting Lord Tremaine with your insolence, the chastisement you so justly merit should quickly be your reward; but it is from your machinations, and those of your sister, whose dishonour you are so willing to hide, by accomplishing mine, that I am indebted for the deprivation of a husband's protecting arm to shield me from insult. Under this roof you cannot remain another instant; therefore do not augment your villainy by refusing to follow my servant, when he receives my commands to show you the door.'

Of course Maria eventually shows herself up in her true colours, and Lord Tremaine learns to esteem his faithful wife as he should. For some time shame prevents him from returning to her, but at length, on seeing in the paper that she has borne him another son, he takes courage. When they finally meet, she sinks into his arms and insensibility, but she soon recovers consciousness, and

the smile that dimpled her beautiful cheek, when she told Tremaine she had nothing to forgive, for his pardon was sealed long before it was demanded, was so obedient, so cheering, that it reached his heart, and rendered her, if possible, still dearer to him.

Her father-in-law is at first implacable, but when Julia and Lord Tremaine kneel before him to implore his forgiveness, he softens:

Nature subdued resentment, and, drawing his children still closer to him, with the hand that was disengaged he laid it on their heads, and in a broken, though impressive, voice, ejaculated, 'God bless my children!'

The concluding sentiments are put in the mouth of Julia:

'Oh! if I had never tasted sorrow, could I have appreciated as they deserve the delightful hours devoted to love and friendship? I fear not. Then let us rejoice at the wisdom of Providence; and, trusting that our errors have hitherto proceeded more from the head than the heart, hope to pass through the remainder of our lives with virtue for our friend, and religion for our guide!'

This story is typical in its setting, plot and treatment of many serials in the penny weekly periodicals. Equally typical of a different kind of story is another *Family Herald* serial, published in 1857. In *Ellen Maynard; or, The Death Wail of the Hawkshaws* we have the fortunes of the friendless orphan girl unexpectedly reduced to poverty and having to rely on her own exertions to make a living. Such a figure was very common among the heroines of romantic fiction at this date, and her trials were invariably severe. Ellen was imprudent enough to take the first position as governess that presented itself. She undertook the education of the son—the boy's age was unspecified—of a Mr. Hawkshaw, who carried her off by night train to the scene of her future employment, having carefully given her a drug to ensure that she should sleep and so be unable to follow their route.

They arrive at a lonely house on a picturesque coast, where Ellen is introduced to a fearsome old beldame, her employer's mother, Lady Clarissa Hawkshaw; to his insane wife; and to her pupil, who proves to be a grown man. Reginald is Mr. Hawkshaw's son by a former marriage to a gipsy who, having quarrelled with her husband, had carrried him off as a baby and brought him up in animal ignorance. He has so far defied all attempts to teach him even to read and write. He is big, strong, handsome and violent, caring for nothing but music and his dog. Despite strong protests at the impropriety of her position Ellen is compelled to stay.

She tames and teaches Reginald, remains unperturbed by the fact that house and grounds are impenetrably locked every night, and carries on unshaken even after the day when her pupil, in a fit of jealous rage, levels a gun at her, wounds her in the arm, and kills his own mother (the long lost gispy), who happens to be crouching outside the schoolroom door. This incident is a lesson to Reginald, who learns to govern his temper, studies with the local clergyman as well as with Ellen, and reads twenty hours a day. Eventually he gets a commission in the regiment of one Frank Willoughby, to whom Ellen is pledged, and follows him to the Crimea. Before departing, he shows Ellen a secret way out of the house, imploring her to use it in case of necessity.

Necessity arises, for that very night Mr. Hawkshaw informs Ellen, with whom he too is violently in love, that his present wife is near death, and proposes that Ellen should succeed her in three days. Meeting with an indignant refusal, he locks Ellen in her room; but she escapes by a secret passage, is forced to hide under the table in a room where her employer and his mother are plotting to poison the insane wife, eventually gets out of the house, wades a swift flowing river, embarks in a rowing boat, and sets out to sea. On looking back she perceives the house to be in flames, and we hear later that both Mr. Hawkshaw and his mother have been burned to death.

Only when in the boat does Ellen give way. She is rescued and cared for, while in the Crimea Reginald becomes Frank Willoughby's friend and exerts an ennobling influence over him. News comes to England that Reginald has been killed, leaving all his property to Ellen. But she refuses to believe he is dead, for she has not heard the death wail of the Hawkshaws. And of course she is quite correct, for Reginald turns up as large as life, and, once satisfied that she no longer cares for Frank, insists on a speedy marriage. The story closes with the happy pair enjoying unexampled felicity. One hopes that they will not find married life too dull.

Another very characteristic tale is *Love Me; Leave Me Not*, a serial by Pierce Egan published in the *London Journal* in 1859 and 1860. Here we encounter another hardy perennial, the tyrannical father who is forcing his daughter into a distasteful marriage. Her sufferings are incredible. She is surrounded by villainy, is misinformed about her lover and believes the slander, is persecuted by the attentions of a deeply depraved suitor, and involved, innocently, in crime of all sorts. The characters foam at the mouth, bite their lips till the blood comes, gnash their teeth, groan and shriek in horrid chorus. In the last episode occur murder, suicide and violent death (two of the characters fall over a precipice while locked in a death-struggle); but in the end virtue is vindicated and vice punished. Similar events are often connected with the traditional castle or abbey (frequently situated in a foreign country), with its apparatus of sliding panels, secret passages, lost wills and priests' holes; against this appropriate background the heroine moves, surrounded by and at last triumphantly surmounting the dangers of drugs, poisoned drinks, brigands, cruel parents, seducers and lunatics.

Yet it is still easy to see why this kind of melodrama was more acceptable than Lloyd's. Highwaymen, robbers, members of the criminal classes have been replaced by bandits, brigands, sinister Italian counts and broken down French aristocrats. These were the kind of characters to be found in stories printed in the expensive magazines. In following their fortunes the readers were transported into another world, and that was probably what most of them wanted of fiction. Burglars and criminals came too close to the reader's ordinary experience. Romance was to be found in the deeds of far away and long ago, or in the lives of persons so exalted by station and wealth that nothing which could be related about them was too fabulous to be credible. The aristocratic element is more obvious in the earlier of the two serials that have been described, but the tendency to describe the remote and the exotic is always there.

This kind of fiction had pitfalls for the writer, and a good many stories show in some degree the imperfect grasp of details of background which is exemplified in a short story from the *Family Herald* called 'The Confessional'. This deals with the unlawful but essentially pure affection of the Lady Isadore de Gonzala for a priest named Bernard de Montalbert. Bernard is represented as

celebrating mass in the evening, while penitents come to confession are called communicants. Isadore in the confessional has
told Bernard of her sinful love, 'and immediately swooned away'.
Bernard, emerging, 'supported in his arms the fainting form of the
most beautiful of God's creatures'. 'He gazed upon the high and
intellectual brow of Isadore with unreserved delight; her finely
chiselled mouth, which defied the sculptor's art to imitate,
ravished his very soul.' To revive her 'he bathed her brow from
the holy font, which then stood near him; and as the refreshing
coolness of the *eau d'esprit* revived her sinking frame, a gentle
murmur escaped her heaving breast'. They part (not, one feels,
a moment too soon), and Bernard leaves for another country,
whither Isadore eventually follows him, enfeebled by suffering.
He visits her on her death-bed, and they expire on the same day.
While few of the stories in these periodicals are quite so super-
latively silly, many of them are shaky in their knowledge of
history, foreign countries, and the usages of polite society.

The short stories in these early periodicals are as a rule less
sensational, but often even more sentimental than the serials.
Many of them are domestic stories of middle-class life. It must be
remembered that in the mid-nineteenth century it was not necessary to drag in family secrets, ghosts, mysterious warnings and
premonitions, scheming villains, drink and drugs in order to
make an exciting story. Life was in some ways very eventful then.
When our credulity is strained by following over and over again
the fortunes of the beautiful girl whose father has lost all in
financial speculation and committed suicide, leaving his penniless
family to contend with a cruel world, we must remember that
this was a period of financial instability, when fortunes were won
and lost with a speed and frequency we can hardly realize. The
famous case of Overend and Gurney and the period of the railway
mania immediately spring to mind. The same consideration
operates in the case of the self-made man, whose struggles are
recounted from the moment his honest childish face and eagerness
to work attract the attention of a wealthy merchant, who be-
friends him. He works his way up to riches, by which time the

benefactor is often bankrupt, and only too glad to bestow on his former protégé the hand of his daughter, previously refused him with scorn. That was the kind of thing that did happen. Similarly, the hazards of sea-travel, the comparative powerlessness of medical science, the frequency of early death, the importance of money in making marriage possible, the wretched disabilities of married women and the dependence of unmarried women, at least in the middle and upper classes, the necessity of long partings when brothers or lovers departed to seek fortunes in India or America, and the strong possibility of receiving no news about them—all these could make the lives of ordinary middle-class people very eventful indeed.

Such events and situations were very powerfully treated in the short stories. In 'The Secret; or, the Dying Confession', a story in the *Family Herald* of 1845, the wealthy Julia St. Clair loves the poor curate Ernest Trevallier. Deterred by the financial gulf that yawns between them, he does not declare himself. Julia pines and falls ill of 'brain fever', and on her death-bed confesses her love, saying: 'But tell me, have I done wrong in avowing to you a passion so pure, so spotless, so holy as mine? No, I am convinced I have not.' With which words she expires. 'After the interment of Julia, Ernest Trevallier was never seen to smile more, and in a few months died of a broken heart.' Another story with the same theme, printed six years later in the same periodical, describes how Blanche Talbot is separated from her lover by the commands of a cruel father. She goes into a decline, and at the end of the story is seated 'supported by pillows, at her organ'. She gradually sinks back in her chair, 'with her eyes closed, apparently in a state of insensibility', till finally her lover forces his way in and comes to her side. He supports her drooping form, and, 'while a smile of unearthly beauty rested on her lips, she died in his arms, gently breathing his name'.

It is true that these periodicals also printed short stories of a more sober kind. Already in Lloyd's weekly papers there had appeared stories which dealt with social problems like the misfortunes of sewing women and the evils of drink, and many of

40188

these, being pirated from America, are interesting for their brisker tone and for depicting women as sometimes capable of action in the face of adversity. And the periodicals that replaced Lloyd's sometimes printed similar stories, where more practical problems were more robustly faced. But generally speaking we find that in this kind of penny fiction the workings of sensibility are unimpeded by the intrusion of sense. Wilting and wasting, swooning and sinking, broken hearts, brain fevers, remorse, decline and early death are the very stuff of which it is made. Beneath exciting serials and sentimental stories alike lies the assumption, never questioned, that romantic love is the chief topic of the writer and the most important thing in life. The author's business is to put obstacles in the way of true love, to surround his radiantly beautiful heroine with dangers and difficulties, and not to abandon her till she is safely married or dead.

IV

'THE MOST POPULAR WRITER OF OUR TIME'

THERE is, however, one writer whose works form an interesting exception to the general run of stories in the most popular penny periodicals of the eighteen-forties and fifties. Mention has already been made of G. W. M. Reynolds, the first editor of the *London Journal*. Reynolds had an interesting life. As a young man he travelled widely on the Continent, where he gained some knowledge of French life and literature, and became an admirer both of the novels of Eugene Sue and of the principles of the revolution of 1789. Between 1848 and 1851 he took a leading part in Chartist agitation, but most of his life was devoted to journalism of one kind or another. He left the *London Journal* to found his own penny weekly, *Reynolds's Miscellany*, at the end of 1846. In 1850 he established a newspaper, which under the title *Reynolds' News* runs to this day. And from 1845 for many years he wrote long novels, which appeared either in penny weekly parts, or else as serials, first in the *London Journal* and later in his *Miscellany*. It is these stories, or rather those written between 1845 and about 1850, that form so strong a contrast with the stories in the other penny periodicals at the time.

Reynolds was an almost unbelievably voluminous writer. A serial, *Mysteries of the Inquisition*, appeared in the first volume of the *London Journal*, to be followed by *Faust;* during 1845 and 1846 there appeared quite independently in penny numbers his very long novel, the *Mysteries of London*. The influence of Sue is at once apparent in the titles. From 1846 his *Miscellany* printed an instalment of one of his serials every week. His *Mysteries of the Court of London* was another huge novel, or rather series of novels, issued between 1849 and 1856. Other works by him continued to appear, but these are the most important and interesting.

All of his stories were long, and all of them were popular. Mayhew tells us that the street-folk regarded Reynolds as 'a trump'; Thackeray, in his lecture 'Comedy and Humour', first delivered in 1852, describes an interview with a bookseller at the Brighton station who attributed Reynolds's unique popularity to the fact that the *Mysteries of the Court of London* lashed the aristocracy. The *Bookseller* in 1868 stated that Reynolds had written more and sold in far greater numbers than Dickens, and in an obituary notice after his death in 1879 the same journal described him as 'the most popular writer of our time'. The notice also describes him as a 'notorious writer'.

Unlike Lloyd, who employed other writers to fill the pages of his publications, and who abandoned penny dreadfuls as soon as his newspaper began to pay, Reynolds kept up his penny weekly and wrote for it during many years. It continued till 1869. As a general rule, writers who make a real success of bad fiction do so because they both enjoy and, in some sense, believe in it. And this was probably the case with Reynolds. What makes his penny stories so interesting to the modern student of popular literature is the detail and gusto with which the early ones describe pain, torture and sexual passion. This kind of writing is a perennial problem to those concerned with public taste and morals, and the control of popular literature today is chiefly designed to eliminate what borders on sadism and pornography. Alone of those who were writing or publishing cheap periodicals in the mid-nineteenth century Reynolds deliberately exploited the market for such literature.

When it is added that some of these earlier stories also reflect his radicalism, the contrast between Reynolds and contemporary writers of cheap fiction is complete.

An excellent example of his work is a serial called *Wagner: the Wehr-Wolf*, which appeared in the first volume of his *Miscellany*. At first sight it might appear merely another tale of love, intrigue and violence, both natural and supernatural, set in sixteenth-century Italy. But, though readers of *The Monk* will be aware of the literary sources of much in the story, it was something very new in penny fiction.

The plot is fundamentally the story of the lovely Nisida,
daughter of a noble Italian family, and her love for Wagner, who
is compelled in return for the gift of youth to become on one day
of every month a dangerous wolf and to roam the country doing
harm. Nisida is jealous by disposition, and commits several crimes
in order to be certain of her lover. Episodes include a description
of a convent where influential people send young females to be
disciplined, sea voyages, wrecks, life on a desert island, scenes in
the life of an apostate Christian in the service of the Sultan, and
the activities of the Inquisition. The story ends with the trans-
formation of Wagner back to his proper form as a very old man,
and his immediate death, followed by that of Nisida.

The first distinction which we notice between this work and
the usual run of things in cheap periodicals is the skill with which
it is written. Reynolds has a fluent, luscious, polysyllabic style
which never fails him. Not only is he never ungrammatical, but
he is almost never awkward or clumsy.

Secondly, the strain of the sensuous of which the *Bookseller*
complained in Reynolds's obituary is indescribably startling.
There is a general tendency in this cheap fiction, as in most popular
fiction, to describe feminine beauty in considerable detail. But
this is a typical description, taken from the *Family Herald* of 1850:

> Alice was one of those tall, aristocratic-looking creatures, who
> notwithstanding a certain slimness, realise, perhaps, the highest ideal
> of female beauty. Her figure was of the lordly Norman type, and
> perfect in its proportions; while every movement was graceful, yet
> dignified. Her face was of that almost divine beauty we see in the
> Beatrice Cenci of Guido. The same dazzling complexion, the same
> blue eyes, the same golden hair. . . . Her countenance, always lovely,
> was now transcendently beautiful, for it glowed with enthusiasm.

The usual run of penny weeklies is thick with these beauties, and
the last sentence is very important. Intellectual and spiritual
qualities were paramount in determining physical beauty.

Now consider this description of Nisida:

> She was attired in deep black; her luxuriant raven hair, no longer
> depending in shining curls, was gathered up in massy bands at the
> sides, and in a knot behind, whence hung a rich veil *that meandered*

over her body's splendidly symmetrical length of limb in such a manner as to aid her attire in shaping rather than hiding the contours of that matchless form. The voluptuous development of her bust was shrouded, not concealed, by the stomacher of black velvet which she wore, and which set off in strong relief the dazzling whiteness of her neck.[1]

When Nisida goes to visit Wagner, who is immured in a dungeon on suspicion of a murder she has herself committed, she disguises herself as a man. This literary device is little used in fiction at this period, but Reynolds avails himself of it often. Nisida's appearance in male attire is fully described:

> Though tall, majestic, and of rich proportions for a woman, yet in the attire of the opposite sex she seemed slight, short, and eminently graceful. The velvet cloak sate so jauntily on her sloping shoulder;—the doublet became her symmetry so well;—and the rich lace-collar was so arranged as to disguise the prominence of the chest—that voluptuous fullness which could not be compressed!

Still later, Nisida is carried away by banditti and then wrecked on a Mediterranean isle. This is a great opportunity for the exercise of Reynolds's peculiar talents. The island is exquisitely beautiful, and productive of every tropical fruit and flower. Nisida roams about it, half-clad and wreathed in flowers, or swims, allowing 'the little wavelets to kiss her snowy bosoms'.

But there is more than the element of the voluptuous (to use a favourite word of Reynolds's) to astonish the reader. By a curious chance, Wagner the Wehr-Wolf is wrecked on the same island as Nisida, and the two become lovers. Illicit love is by no means unusual in nineteenth-century literature, but its treatment by Reynolds is at this date unique. His lovers, the women as well as the men, *enjoy* themselves. They may not escape punishment (though often they do [2]) but neither do they drag out a miserable

---

[1] The italics are in the original.
[2] An example of a fallen woman who comes to a good end is Diana Arlington, a character in the *Mysteries of London*, who at the end of Vol. II marries the Earl of Warrington and lives happy and respectable ever after. She has been earlier described as a woman who gives herself no airs, never excites her lover's jealousy by actual or pretended infidelity, and is his confidant and adviser in business matters—'There was a great amount of real friendship and good feeling between those two'.

existence, tormented by the reproaches of conscience and each other, ostracized by society, cut off from family and friends, and at length, the females at any rate, sinking into an early grave, a prey to remorse. The exemplar of such stories is *East Lynne*. So clear is the conscience of the mistress of Nisida's father (who was of course a Count) that she attended mass regularly throughout their amour. No special point is made of this, and it does not seem to be a part of Reynolds's anti-clericalism, merely an indication of ideas with which his travels and reading had doubtless made him familiar.

This elastic attitude to immorality in the narrow sense of the word extends at times to its wider aspects. It is true that on the whole Reynolds's murderers, swindlers, robbers, seducers, and criminals generally, come to a bad end, but they have a wonderful run for their money first, and sometimes retribution is brief. Nisida, after committing two murders and plotting mercilessly against the girl who is loved by her brother, not to mention the love-affair with Wagner, repents only on her death-bed, when we are assured by the mysterious Rosicrucian who attends her that all is well. Even a single case of such lenience in a world of rigid and clear-cut moral distinctions is remarkable.

Reynolds's taste for the voluptuous is reasonably restrained in the serials published in the *Miscellany*. In the *Mysteries of London*, however, and still more in the earlier volumes of the *Mysteries of the Court of London*, both of which first appeared in penny numbers, there is a good deal of the semi-pornographic. Examples are to be found in the numerous scenes in the *Mysteries of the Court of London* which take place in the superior brothel disguised as the establishment of a fashionable milliner. Here most of the work-women are enchanting prostitutes, while others are innocent victims about to be enticed to their doom. George IV pursues many of his amours in these surroundings, and scenes of seduction and passion abound. Some of these have their amusing side, as when a chapter ends as follows: 'And as he glued his lips, hot and parched with the fever of burning lust, to her delicious mouth, her senses abandoned her—and she remained powerless and inanimate in his arms!' The next chapter, part of the same instalment, begins: 'Grieved as we are to leave the reader in a state of suspense relative to the issue of the adventure of Pauline Clarendon and the Prince of Wales, we must nevertheless break the thread of that episode for a short space and return to Covent Garden Theatre.'

Another characteristic of Reynolds's work which comes as a shock after even the most lurid of the penny dreadfuls is the description of cruelty. The first instalment of the *Mysteries of the Inquisition* gave a detailed account of half-naked victims of the Holy Office being scourged, and of the application of torture by water to a young woman whose offence is that her sister has become a Lutheran. We are carefully told that the victim has just had a baby. The details include the description of the 'wooden horse', the special couch on which she was laid, the tightening of cords binding her so that they disappeared, embedded in flesh, and the actual torture (this is followed immediately by an article decrying the early penny dreadfuls as 'appealing exclusively to the passions, or, rather, the excitabilities of men', and proclaiming that the *London Journal* will be subjected to the wholesome restraints of reason and the moral principle). In *Wagner* the inquisition appears again, and a good deal is made of the torture and death of one, fair but frail, stretched naked on the rack before the eyes of her captive lover and her exulting husband. At times also there are in the *Miscellany* articles giving information on subjects which we would prefer not to know about, as one with a detailed illustration and a full account of guillotining, and another describing instruments of torture. The translation of Sue's *Mysteries of the People* in the 1850 volume contains some scenes of torture, also illustrated. Reynolds's serials in later volumes of the *Miscellany* are inoffensive enough in this respect, but the *Mysteries of London*, also one of his earlier works, is full of cruelty. In Volume I we find, among other things, horrible descriptions of the ill-treatment of children, including blinding them to make them useful beggars; a detailed account of a hanging; and an account of the slow and systematic murder of a child for the sake

A Heroine's End. Fleeing from the embraces of a royal personage, one of
Reynolds's unfortunate young women falls into space.

of 'burial money'. Reynolds's very skill as a writer makes this
kind of thing peculiarly disagreeable. That such things happened
is only too true, but we can bear to read them only if they are
described with compassion. Reynolds may have felt this, but his
florid and declamatory style does not convey it.

His hostility to the clergy extends from the dissenting parson
who gets so drunk that he has to be conveyed home in a wheel-
barrow, is voted a piece of plate by his congregation, and increases
its numbers to the extent of three children by three different
servant girls, to the gaol chaplain who is seen through the eyes of
the hangman:

> 'Last time there was an execution, the Chaplain says to me, says
> he, "Smithers, I don't think you had your hand nicely in this
> morning"?—"Don't you, sir?" says I.—"No," says he: "I've seen
> you do it more genteel than that."—"Well, Sir," says I, "I'll do my
> best to please you next time."—"Ah! do, there's a good fellow,
> Smithers," says the Chaplain; and off he goes to breakfast with the
> Sheriffs and governor, a-smacking his lips at the idea of the cold
> fowl and ham that he meant to pitch into.'

A major part in the plot of the *Mysteries of London* is played by
a fashionable clergyman named Reginald Tracy, who is seduced
by a fashionable lady. He thereupon becomes a complete libertine,
not confining his attentions to any one woman. His meeting with
one of the less consistently respectable female characters in the
book gives rise to the following:

> At a glance his eyes scanned the fair form of Ellen from head to
> foot; and his imagination was instantly fired with the thoughts of
> her soft and swelling charms—those graceful undulations which were
> all her own, and needed no artificial aids to improve the originals of
> nature!

Later the same gentleman peers at Ellen through the keyhole of
the 'bathing-room', but he is interrupted before she is completely
undressed. We are not surprised when he comes to a bad end.

Similar attacks on the clergy are found throughout the eight
volumes of the *Mysteries of the Court of London*, the events of
which vary in date from the late eighteenth century to more or

4

less the time of writing. The grossest avarice and lust are thinly disguised, while the threat of exposure reduces the reverend gentlemen to pulp. A more rational indictment assails the indifference of the clergy to the condition of the common people:

> Oh! what have the myriad fat and bloated pastors done for the population that swarms in those frightful neighbourhoods? . . . If a missionary of Religion be ever encountered in such places, be well assured that he belongs not to the Established Church, which is so extravagantly paid by compulsion, but to the sphere of Dissent, which is sustained by voluntary contributions.

Finally, Reynolds's radicalism. This is shown in the *Miscellany*, in articles at first and later more frequently in answers to correspondents. In a serial like *Wagner: the Wehr-Wolf*, with setting and events as remote as possible from those of daily life, there is no scope for it, but one like *The Slaves of England. No. 1. The Seamstress* (published in the *Miscellany* in 1850) is a good vehicle for the expression of social and political ideas. Reynolds is very disturbed about the wrongs of seamstresses—his blood boils repeatedly as he chronicles the sufferings of 'Virginia' and her colleagues. (It is a pity that the undoubted righteousness of his cause, a cause taken up by people like Shaftesbury, should be obscured by Reynolds's artificial and declamatory style, so that it is hard to avoid suspicions about his sincerity.)

When Virginia goes to sew in private houses, she is said seldom or never to receive considerate treatment, but to be hurried on with her work when she is feeling ill and to be exposed to the insulting attentions of the young men in the families. She dies at last of overwork. The Duke of Belmont, the weak and wicked father of her faithful suitor, commits suicide; the suitor, having announced that 'Hope is to me like a withered flower—and despair spreads its vampyre-like wings over my heart!' engages in a duel with the man who has contrived his father's downfall, both parties are killed, and the Duchess dies of grief and shock. Thus are demonstrated the general perfidy of the aristocracy (the honest lover always excepted) and the nobility of the poor.

Like Reynolds's *Miscellany*, the *Mysteries of London* and the *Mysteries of the Court of London* are active in the onslaught on the arictocracy which Mayhew's costermonger and Thackeray's bookseller saw as the secret of Reynolds's popularity. The attack in the *Mysteries of London* is on constituted authority of every kind, and not only members of the governing classes but all government institutions are represented as corrupt. For example, there occurs a minute description of the illegal censorship of letters carried on from 'The Black Chamber' in the main post office of St. Martin-le-Grand; horror of the workhouse is consistently instilled and the whole system of justice is attacked. The Home Secretary's charge to a newly appointed magistrate runs as follows: 'You must always shield the upper classes as much as possible; and . . . bring out the misdeeds of the lower orders in the boldest relief.'

But if government is an organized conspiracy of the rich against the poor, the poor as individuals in these books are not idealized, in spite of Reynolds's outbursts of glowing sentiment on their behalf as a class. They are in most cases represented as miserably debased, venal and corrupt, rather than as sublime, generous and noble-hearted. Reynolds's whole view of human nature and society is fundamentally cynical. It is impossible, in reading him, to avoid the conviction that he relishes the description of vice and crime. But he freely proclaims a high moral purpose. Towards the end of the second volume of the *Mysteries of London* he asks: 'And shall we be charged with vanity, if we declare that never until now has the veil been so rudely torn aside, nor the corruptions of London been so boldly laid bare?' The epilogue of the same volume forestalls objections to the sordidness of this revelation by claiming that the good as well as the bad has been described, and the bad only that it may be condemned. 'In exposing the hideous deformity of vice, have we not studied to develop the witching beauty of virtue?' he cries. In other words, he muckrakes only to reform.

Yet it is with a certain regret that the modern reader sees the qualities which make his work so strongly individual disappear from Reynolds's work, which in his later years was not much different from that of other writers of penny fiction. In his earlier days he was at least original. The reason why it has been necessary to discuss in such detail his luscious style, his descriptions of the sensuous and the cruel, his strong radical and anti-clerical attitude, is just that they are unique. Considering their enormous success, the fact that they were not imitated speaks volumes for either the moral standards or the incompetence of other writers of popular fiction at the time. Were they deterred from attempting the imitation, and was Reynolds himself induced to change his style by the attack on popular literature that began somewhere about 1847? It is certain that the later volumes of the *Mysteries of the Court of London* abandon the dramatic exposure of the dishonesty, profligacy and intemperance of George IV for sensational stories involving fictitious characters in more conventional courses of embezzlement, murder, abduction and the rest. And the later volumes of the *Miscellany* differ much from the earlier ones. Reynolds himself contributed mild historical serials, such as *Margaret: or, the Discarded Queen*, and *Mary Stuart, Queen of Scots*. Gone are the voluptuous houris who lend such life to his earlier works, and in their place we meet niminy-piminy little creatures like the two girls who are described respectively as 'a sweet fair-haired young creature of seventeen, and whose beauty was of the most interesting and exquisite description', and 'a superbly handsome, fine-grown, dark-haired damsel of about eighteen'. Even when his heroines are up to their old tricks and disguise themselves in male attire, it is no longer the same thing, as is shown by the following:

> We must nevertheless pause for a moment to remark how well that page's apparel became the slight, lithe, and elegant figure which it invested. The redundant ebon tresses were gathered up in such a way that the greater portion of their mass was concealed by the black velvet cap; while the plume, as above stated, served to shade the countenance. Gualdi could not help thinking that the lady looked as interesting and attractive in male apparel as she was ravishing in her own more appropriate garb.

Scenes of cruelty, debauchery and vice seldom occur, and if they do they are described in a conventional and colourless style. It seems possible that Reynolds was influenced in making these changes by the increasingly frequent attacks on the morality of cheap literature, and by the example of a better class of cheap periodical.

V

THE MORAL ISSUE

THESE early attacks on popular literature were characterized by a combination of moral fervour and ignorance which is usual in similar attacks today. But all the same, from 1847 they were so strong that they seem gradually to have forced Reynolds, for example, to change his tone and style, and from about that time also there began to appear new periodicals which tried to provide better popular reading than had hitherto been available at a really low price. This shows quite clearly what can be done in this field by the pressure of public opinion. Such voluntary censorship has great dangers, but these are at their least when the literature attacked has no faintest pretension to artistic merit. In this particular case the effect of a fairly silly public outcry was good. A writer like Reynolds had to conform to better standards, and on the other hand a man like Dickens accepted the implicit challenge to provide better cheap literature, producing his periodical *Household Words*.

Even before 1847 the existence of a special literature of the poor was realized, and its quality sometimes criticized. In 1840, the *Athenaeum*, reviewing a novel by Mrs. Gore, discussed the greatly increased demand for fiction and asserted that sensational literature was needed to arouse the sympathies of readers who were absorbed in the struggle for existence. For them 'are produced the atrocities of the Newgate school, the adventures of buccaneers, the sea novels, and other types of coarse and exciting adventure'. In the same year a periodical of a very different type, a short-lived little *Halfpenny Magazine*, published a letter from a correspondent attacking 'the garbage which is daily and weekly served up by the periodical press—aye, and eagerly swallowed by the people, too'. The vein in which this writer continues is one that is to become

46

only too familiar in ten years time, strongly condemnatory but
totally unspecific. In his opinion,

> Trashy tales, or horrid stories, filled with murders, assassinations,
> rapes, seductions, and other gross and exciting matter, are eagerly
> sought after, and swallowed, administering to the depraved appetite
> of an ignorant and perverse generation; whilst wholesome mental
> nutriment is left untouched and unheeded.

In 1846, announcing the discontinuance of *Knight's Penny
Magazine* (the successor of the original *Penny Magazine*) Knight
lashed out at his rivals. These are the people who

> are carrying out the principle of cheap weekly sheets to the disgrace
> of the system, and who appear to have got some considerable hold
> upon the less informed of the working people, and especially upon
> the young. There are manufactories in London whence hundreds of
> reams of vile paper and printing issue weekly; where large bodies of
> children are employed to arrange types, at the wages of shirt-makers,
> from copy furnished by the most ignorant, at the wages of scaven-
> gers. In truth, such writers, if they deserve the name of writers, *are*
> scavengers. All the garbage that belongs to the history of crime and
> misery is raked together, to diffuse a moral miasma through the land,
> in the shape of the most vulgar and brutal fiction.

Against such competition, journals such as his have little chance
to reach the least informed readers, who most need sound knowledge but instead are reading 'such things as *Newgate, A Romance,
The Black Mantle; or, the Murder at the Old Jewry, The Spectre at the
Hall, The Feast of Blood, The Convict,* and twenty others'. This is a
direct attack on penny dreadfuls of the Salisbury Square type; *The
Feast of Blood* is the alternative title to Prest's novel, *Varney the
Vampire*, which was published in penny parts by Lloyd, and *Newgate*
also seems to have been by Prest.

But the first really comprehensive attack took the form of three
articles by Hepworth Dixon in the *Daily News* of 1847. In these
he drew the attention of educated readers to the existence of a
submerged literature, possessing 'its own system of morals and
merits', widely different from those of 'the higher and better
known offsprings [sic] of the press'. Dixon emphasized its extent
and influence in the following words:

The man who declared that any one might make the laws of a country—so that he was permitted to write its popular ballads—probably did not exaggerate the power of the people's literature in producing and determining the national character.

He therefore set about giving an account of the literature of the poorest and least educated members of the reading public. And while the fine frenzy of moral indignation he expresses is but too typical of the sort of thing that was about to spring up on all sides, Dixon's articles had at least the merit of speaking out and naming what they attacked. Very few indeed of the many people who expressed similar views had the courage to name the objects of their attacks, frequently under a revolting pretence that to do so would encourage a prurient curiosity.

Unfortunately, his courage and that of the *Daily News* were not equalled by his knowledge of the subject. Where what he says about Lloyd's publications can be tested (not all of those he names survive), he is mistaken. He says that the dozen serials issued weekly at a penny each by the Salisbury Square press all turn upon 'scenes of robbery and seduction'. The robber or pirate is a hero, the betrayed and culpable heroine a martyr, and events 'a succession of sickly but exciting scenes'—'theft, seduction, violence, adultery, and murder'. In them 'peculation, seduction, and adultery form the staple of the materials which are worked up into amusement and instruction for the masses'. All Lloyd's publications give to crime 'an impress of reckless and successful adventure'.

Not all of this is true, and in particular the statement that crime in Salisbury Square fiction is allowed to pay is false. Lloyd himself claimed in the preface to the first volume of his *Penny Weekly Miscellany* to 'maintain the high majesty of virtue over the turbulence of vice'. There is little gloating over or relish of any kind of vice in his publications; virtue is universally triumphant, and wrong doing is punished by obloquy and ruin in this world, by threats also of eternal torment in the next. And if the mere description of criminal action and character were at fault, what about the enormous popularity of works by Dickens, Ainsworth and Bulwer? Charges that Lloyd's stories condoned female unchastity were equally unfounded. It is true that his heroines sometimes love not wisely but too well (to use their own language), but they suffer deeply for their faults, and the connection between sin and suffering is made very clear. One erring woman, telling her own story, says: 'The being who has once strayed from the path of virtue, alas! can never again be permanently happy'; and this attitude is consistently put forward.

Dixon is more accurate in his attack on Reynolds's stories, which are criticized for dealing less in the criminal, more in the licentious and blasphemous than those of Lloyd. They

> poison the very fountains of human life, by confounding conscience, confusing the sense of right and wrong, and by corrupting and inflaming those passions whose regulation and co-ordination with duty constitute the basis of morals, and offer the only guarantee for the peace and well-being of the social body.

Reynolds's Miscellany and serials like *Faust* and *Wagner: the Wehr-Wolf* he regarded as the least noxious, being no worse than much of the literature of the day which aspired to higher rank. But the translations from the French (mostly of Eugène Sue) were specially disgusting, while of the *Mysteries of London* nothing too bad could be said:

> To such of our readers as have toiled through Eugène Sue's dullest and most popular work, 'The Mysteries of Paris', *The Mysteries of London*, now lying before us, will be sufficiently explained. If it be possible to conceive of anything more miserable, murderous, immoral, and reprehensible than the succession of scenes which constitute that darling of the Parisian boulevards—that grosser conception will give an idea of what the mysteries of the modern Babylon are like.

But there was worse yet. The third article refers darkly to 'a mass of impurity and corruption which we dare not touch'. The writer will not satisfy a prurient curiosity by naming examples of this, and so we are left in the dark about what he means. Presumably he is talking of what are described in the fourth volume of *London Labour and the London Poor*, illegal books, banned by the

Immoral Publications Act, which were said to be on the decrease, but were still hawked about by people who got them from 'the filthy cellars of Holywell Street'. There seems certainly to have been a huge trade in pornographic literature, leading in 1857 to the passing of the Obscene Publications Bill, which strengthened the hands of the police by making summary jurisdiction possible in such cases.

This third article ended on a note of hope. Already, as education advanced, grosser literature was decreasing in quantity, while certain very popular periodicals were somewhat better than those discussed. Of these he mentioned the *Family Herald*, the *London Journal*, and a very similar paper, the *London Pioneer*, as exhibiting a morality not quite diabolical, sentiments not incurably depraved, and characters much above 'the gross personages of the *Penny Sunday Times*'. The *Family Herald*, a purely domestic magazine, was decidedly the least offensive of its class, though the correspondence column came in for a slap. The editor states that he gets a hundred letters a day, mainly from young females. 'Where can be the mothers of these simple creatures while they are placing themselves in such unmaidenly communication with strangers—of the other sex, too?'

Hepworth Dixon's attack on popular literature has been described in some detail because it embodies the views and arguments of many writers in the next few years. The keynote of the attack was *moral*. Literature forms character, and is to be judged by its influence in this direction rather than by any aesthetic criterion. Not a word has Dixon to say, in connection with Salisbury Square fiction, about clumsy plot construction, characterization stereotyped at the lowest level, and a style that combines the high-flown with the ungrammatical; and he is equally indifferent to the superior literary quality of Reynolds's writings. The same is true of the frequent statements about popular literature to be found in the following years. The *Athenaeum* and the *Examiner* supported the *Daily News*. The 1849 report of the Select Committee on Public Libraries included a few disappointingly vague but strongly condemnatory references to the literature of the lower orders. Dickens, beginning the first number of *Household Words* in 1850 with 'A Preliminary Word', referred to certain popular periodicals as 'Bastards of the Mountain, draggled fringe on the Red Cap, Panders to the basest passions of the lowest natures—whose existence is a national reproach'. The reference is almost certainly to the radicalism of Reynolds's *Mysteries of London*. And the section on prostitution in the extra volume of *London Labour and the London Poor* sees penny and halfpenny romances as a 'very fruitful source of early demoralization'. It continues:

> The ruin of many girls is commenced by reading the low trashy wishy-washy cheap publications that the news-shops are now gorged with, and by devouring the hastily-written, immoral, stereotyped tales about the sensualities of the upper classes, the lust of the aristocracy, and the affection that men about town—noble lords, illustrious dukes, and even princes of the blood—are in the habit of imbibing for maidens of low degree 'whose face is their fortune'.

Girls wait for the duke; when he does not turn up, they are content to receive the immodest advances of someone in their own walk of life, 'demoralized by the trash that has corrupted their minds'. This seems another obvious reference to Reynolds, not to his radicalism but to the love stories, especially those in the earlier volumes of the *Mysteries of the Court of London*.

These criticisms are only some of those that appeared, all sharing the same moralistic but not religious tone. From 1850 a more specifically religious point of view was expressed in many of the attacks on penny fiction. A doughty champion in the cause of a purified penny press was a Miss Fanny Mayne, who wrote several articles on this subject which appeared in the *Englishwoman's Magazine* between 1850 and 1852. 'The working classes of the country,' she wrote in 1850, 'both in agricultural and manufacturing districts, are, to a great extent, a *reading people; a reading* and a *thinking people!*' They have their own press, newspapers, magazines, periodicals and novels, and will sacrifice even food to buy them—'so true is the saying that *reading is a sensual gratification;* though not always the most refined of sensual gratifications'. The effect of such reading is simple: 'Tales of imagination, then, that deal in murders, and in other species of iniquity, lead to the actual commission of similar sins.'

Nothing could be more clear cut. Yet Miss Mayne was not altogether naïve in her view of literature and its effects, for next year, in 'A Letter on Providing Proper Literature for the Working Classes' she wrote:

> Wherever you draw a tear, or make the cheek flush, or the heart palpitate, there you educate; and why may not the tear be made to flow, the cheek to flush, and the heart to palpitate, by other descriptions than those which would show us 'St. Giles' oppressed by 'St. James'?

This attack on Douglas Jerrold's novel, *St Giles and St. James*, which first appeared as a serial in his *Shilling Magazine* from 1845 till 1847, was paralleled by an onslaught on *Household Words* made in a little pamphlet entitled *The Perilous Nature of the Penny Periodical Press* (Miss Mayne was strong on alliteration), which she published in 1851. While Dickens's cheap weekly was regarded as standing apart from the others, by reason of the great talents of the author, yet

> there is scarcely a work in the land that tends more to separate class from class, or to make the poor man feel that he is oppressed and overborne by the rich, and that the laws and institutions, and authorities of the country are *against him* and *for them*.

Chambers and Knight too were blamed for basing the education they gave in their periodicals 'merely on moral, and not on religious and Christian principles. Morality, as apart from religion, is nothing better than heathenism in a purified form.'

This attitude will be recognized by the social historian as perfectly consistent with the tenets of strict evangelicalism. Indeed, compared with views expressed in the *British Mother's Magazine*, which printed fairly frequent articles on the subject of 'light reading' between 1851 and 1855, Miss Fanny Mayne's are mildly rational. For the *British Mother's Magazine*, a periodical which put forward the most stringent view of all moral and religious topics, including frightful pronouncements on the education of children, held quite simply that all fiction was to be avoided. It wasted time, unfitted the reader for better literature, and imparted false ideas of life, stimulating without feeding the mind and imagination, and blunting the sensibilities to real horrors because they are less extravagant than fictitious ones. Spine-chilling stories were told of the effects of novel reading—for example, of a man who became so addicted to the vice that he pursued it night and day till it undermined his constitution, and 'now the grass is grown over his grave'. Naturally, the habit was to be deprecated when it extended to the poor, and in 1853 appeared an attack on the deadly trash that is finding its way into Christian homes,

> not in the *least* insinuating dangerous form, through the numerous domestic periodicals of the day. On the one page you will find receipts for making Bath buns, tooth powder, clearing out ink spots, &c., and on the other a highly coloured love story; which, if weighed in the balance of strict Christian principle, would be found miserably wanting.

When Miss Mayne established her own penny periodical, the *True Briton*, it contained fiction. For she realized that people wanted fiction and intended to have it, and that the best that could be done was to provide it in an unobjectionable, if possible a definitely beneficial form. But even in the *True Briton* the fight continued, and the poor *Family Herald* came in for yet another, this time well-informed attack. For clearly it is one of those which

> furnish tales of the 'Novel' tribe, with scraps of useful and scientific information, and moral and religious lucubrations, such as they are. The tales, with some exceptions, are of the most trashy, wishy-washy kind, so unlike real life, that no persons of common sense, I should think, could endure to read them. This class is chiefly objectionable in not at least tacitly recognising the Bible as the standard of moral and religious truth. The religious sentiments held forth are of every variety, and sufficiently absurd and ridiculous in kind. Deism, Pantheism, Universalism, and a great many other isms, have here their propounders. I have often wondered where they got their various systems from. . . . The only evidence of their truth, which those who put them forth could offer, would be, I am sure, 'Them's my sentiments—that's what I thinks'.

The evangelical conviction that all that was not with them was against them led naturally to the rejection of the great mass of cheap literature which reflected the vaguely Christian position and broad humanitarian feeling of a writer like Dickens, and indeed of many people who were writing for periodicals like the *Family Herald* and the *London Journal*. It was not just that certain of their views on social problems were unacceptable to prosperous middle-class people. Still more fundamental was the conviction that morality is not enough. Perfect propriety of feeling and behaviour are nothing without conversion. The revulsion of educated people from the popular literature of the eighteen-forties led therefore in two directions. On the one hand there appeared a number of new periodicals which claimed to be morally superior to those that had preceded them; on the other appeared those that claimed to be superior on the strictest religious grounds. The next two chapters will consider these new developments.

VI

'A PURIFIED PENNY PRESS'—I

ABOUT half the cheap periodicals that first appeared between 1846 and 1856 and established themselves at all were sponsored by religious organizations, or reflected positive religious opinions. The other half included works of the quality of *Household Words*, *Eliza Cook's Journal*, and *Cassell's Illustrated Family Paper*.

The very titles of the works in these groups are significant. Publications reflecting evangelical views include the *Churchman's Monthly Penny Magazine*, the *Mother's Friend*, the *True Briton*, the *Leisure Hour*, the *Sunday at Home*, and the *Family Paper*. The *Penny Post* was the High Church equivalent of the *Churchman's Penny Magazine*. The Society for Promoting Christian Knowledge established the *Home Friend* on less sectarian lines. Publications without any specific religious affiliation included the *Family Economist*, *Eliza Cook's Journal*, the *Family Friend*, the *Home Circle*, *Household Words*, the *Home Companion*, *Cassell's Illustrated Family Paper*, the *Home Magazine*, and the *British Workman*. There is no mistaking the emphasis on the domestic affections and on loyalty to church and country.

The people responsible for the purified penny press of the late forties and early fifties were, with one or two exceptions, anxious not so much to support the poor man in his struggle against the rich as to improve him, and to help him to improve himself. The new periodicals contain many stories and articles about the sufferings of poor people, but these are attributed not to the wickedness of others, but to their own deficiencies, either the lack of the solid virtues of industry, thrift, temperance, punctuality and early rising, or to the lack of true religion. The relentless persistence with which this message is conveyed makes these periodicals very interesting as revealing middle-class early Victorian attitudes to the poor. While the penny dreadfuls and

the stories in penny papers like the *Family Herald* have a literary
interest as debased copies of the Gothic and sentimental novels,
stories in papers like *Eliza Cook's Journal* and the *Leisure Hour* are
interesting because they reflect the actual convictions of their
writers about men in relation to society and to God.

Let us first consider the periodicals which lacked any specifically
religious motive or point of view, yet were more or less consciously designed to provide cheap popular literature of a better quality
than most that had yet appeared. Of these, nine have been
mentioned at the beginning of this chapter. All of them lasted at
least four or five years, some very much longer, so that they all
must have met the taste of a fair number of readers.

The *Family Economist* and the *Family Friend* appeared respectively in 1848 and 1849, and in 1860 were amalgamated. Their
objects were fundamentally alike, to promote 'the moral,
physical, and domestic improvement of the industrious classes'.
While the few stories they print contain many vaguely reverential
references to religion, these two periodicals really concentrate on
inculcating the virtues of industry, prudence, cleanliness and
economy. Both exclude politics, social problems and current
affairs, and instead print advice on cooking, cottage gardening
and farming, beekeeping, making over old clothes, and so on.
Earlier periodicals like the *Family Herald* had done nothing so
thorough and detailed along these lines. Clearly these little
monthly papers are in this respect the prototypes of a great tribe
of modern magazines, with their strong emphasis on the arts and
activities that centre in the home.

In contrast, *Eliza Cook's Journal*, which first appeared in 1849,
though edited by a woman was not at all concerned with the
domestic arts. Neither did it contain very much fiction. In reading
it, one gains a strong impression that it was largely written by
women of serious, liberal, but somewhat restricted interests. Like
most cheap popular periodicals it avoided politics and religion.
But it lacked also the articles on scientific, historical, and geo-
graphical subjects which were so conspicuous, for example, in
Chambers' Journal and *Cassell's Illustrated Family Paper*. There were

The Reformed Drunkard and an Old Companion. One of a series of drawings from the *True Briton* depicting the stages of a mid-Victorian progress from Hogarthian depravity to preternatural piety.

none of the features on which depended so much of the popularity of the average cheap weekly—the illustrations, correspondence, puzzles, problems, and jokes. *Eliza Cook's Journal* was mainly concerned with social conditions, specially so far as they affected women and children, and specially in connection with female emigration; with education, literature, and descriptions of natural beauty; and with the advocacy of certain qualities like tolerance between classes, contentment, cheerfulness and industry. It printed a good deal of poetry, notably the productions of the editor, and frequently had a column for children. This last, though firmly moral, usually displayed a tone that was advanced for its time, being generally lively and pleasant, and often showing a lighter touch, as when fairies are introduced to work reformation in faulty characters.

Less than half the space was taken up by fiction. The stories, specially in the first year or two, were consistent in tone with the sober realism of the articles and sketches. Most of them were placed in a modern setting, quite half of them dealt with themes other than romantic love, and the characters were never members of the aristocracy, whether native or foreign. While the literary standard is not high, many of the plots are given vitality and interest by their earnestness of purpose. It may be argued that this latter quality is often a great enemy to artistic success, but any evidence of concern with real problems is wonderfully welcome in a wilderness of triviality. A hatred of strong drink, an interest in female emigration, a general concern for the poor, if felt deeply enough, lend vitality to the stories they inspire.

The Glass of Gin,[1] a serial in six parts which appeared in 1849, is absurd enough in all conscience, as far as the plot is concerned. It tells the story of two half-sisters who, left in poverty at their father's death, go to seek their fortune in London. One is all perfection, and after many tribulations achieves an excellent position as a governess, and eventually the hand of her charges' uncle. The other begins to drink, and sinks lower and lower in her

[1] The author is 'Silverpen', Miss Eliza Meteyard. She also wrote *Lucy Dean; the Noble Needlewoman*, and *Mrs. Dumple's Cooking School.*

5

attempts to get money, disposes of all the bits of property they have salvaged, tries the saintly Alice to the utmost, and eventually expires in a fearful frenzy. Alice swoons frequently, the little boys she teaches caress her, and their grandfather weeps quite often, whenever he is particularly happy. The same old gentleman, though deeply grateful to Alice for all she has done for his grandsons, yet is easily convinced that she is responsible for and a partner in her sister's depravity, and she takes no rational steps to convince him otherwise. The characterization is completely stereotyped. Yet the story has life. The very block capitals in which GIN appears on every page—ACCURSED, BRUTALIZING GIN —give it force. The problem of drunkenness is real, and the writer's feelings about it are real, however ridiculous the story through which she tries to express them.

Lucy Dean; the Noble Needlewoman is another short serial with a theme, the desirability of female emigration, which is often developed in the articles and stories of *Eliza Cook's Journal*. The events of this particular story suggest a familiarity with the work of Caroline Chisholm and her Family Colonization Loan Society. There is no very obvious similarity between the character of Mrs. Chisholm and that of Mary Austen in the story—Mary Austen is young and unmarried and has never been to Australia—but their motives are alike. Mary Austen is anxious to help poor but respectable Englishwomen (of whom Lucy Dean is the type in the story), and to improve social conditions in Australia by encouraging the right type of female emigrant. Lucy is a sewing woman who drags out a miserable existence in bitter poverty, but who is befriended by Mary and encouraged to save towards her passage money to Australia. When her ship arrives there, the women are received in Adelaide and helped by a committee of ladies. Lucy gets a good position as housekeeper to a mining supervisor, and by her work and influence transforms the lives of the miners. She persuades them to subscribe to a fund for providing passages to Australia for respectable women, and later returns to England to forward the work of an association for assisting the emigration of women, then goes back to Australia

and marries her original employer. Mary Austen herself goes to
Australia, where she marries a man who has long sympathized
with her work; Lucy, Mary, female emigrants, miners and all
live happy ever after.

This story lacks the salient absurdities of *The Glass of Gin*,
though the rosy picture it paints of colonial life might be misleading in a more insidious way. On the other hand, the modern
reader is attracted by the common sense which advocates that
women should leave grim poverty or genteel beggary (for the
appeal is by no means to working-class women only) for a land
of opportunity. There is also the courageous insistence that women
themselves should take a hand in improving conditions for their
fellows. No attempt is made to analyse a political and economic
system which makes such expedients necessary, to apportion
blame or to suggest a cure, but an immediate remedy is seen and
seized upon.

The same readiness to ignore abstract matters of cause and to
suggest practical solutions for social problems is seen in yet
another serial, *Mrs. Dumple's Cooking School*. In this story a group
of charity school girls are taught plain cooking on both a large
and a small scale; the raw materials seem to be provided by
charity, and the girls end up by making hot meals for several
Ragged Schools and a model lodging house. Into this refreshingly
matter-of-fact narrative—a number of good recipes are incorporated in the story—intrude elements of melodrama. There is a
recognition scene in which a small girl befriended by Mrs.
Dumple is claimed by her wealthy father, and overpowering
evidences of virtue rewarded when eleven of the original twelve
charity girls are married on the same day, all very suitably, each
wearing a silver-hued satin gown, the gift, along with a Bible and
£100 apiece, of the original patron of the venture. But not even
all this rubbish can disguise the benevolence which would issue,
not in indiscriminate charity, but in helping the unfortunate to
help themselves.

These are examples of what is most individual in the fiction
printed in *Eliza Cook's Journal* in its early stages. There was of

course from the beginning much that was written merely to amuse, reflecting the conventional morality of cheerfulness, modesty, hard work, disinterestedness, charity, and so on. But apparently there were financial difficulties, and in 1854 an attempt was made to save the *Journal* by dropping these vigorous and often realistic stories and replacing them by translations and by tales of counts and castles. There was still much that was sensible and lively, but much also that was sentimental and silly. *The Recollections of Mrs Hester Taffetas* included seven episodes, all but one of which involve such topics as seduction, illegitimacy, suicide, murder, substitution of children, and death from unrequited affection. It is a far cry from this kind of thing to the noble needlewoman cooking for South Australian miners. It seems probable that Eliza Cook hoped that the change would increase the sales of the periodical—the proprietors of the *Family Herald* knew what would sell. But the change of policy was unsuccessful, and in the same year the *Journal* ceased to appear.

Household Words began in 1850 and had something in common with *Eliza Cook's Journal*. Both were weeklies a little more expensive than those designed for the very poor (*Household Words* cost twopence, *Eliza Cook's Journal* a penny-halfpenny); both were bent on exploiting a well known name in their struggle to attract readers; and there was considerable similarity in their contents. Both spurned the facile attractions of riddles, puzzles, illustrations, correspondence columns, and so on. Both were keenly interested in social problems, and in emigration as a solution for them. Both gave less space to fiction than to articles and sketches. The difference lies in the quality and scope of the latter, and in the quality of their fiction.

Dickens's hope in starting *Household Words* was to provide cheap and popular reading matter which should be better than most of what was available, and which should in a sense take the place of sternly improving works like the defunct *Penny Magazine*. But, as Forster tells us,

> There was to be no mere utilitarian spirit; with all familiar things, but especially those repellent on the surface, something was to be

connected that should be fanciful or kindly; and the hardest workers were to be taught that their lot is not necessarily excluded from the sympathies and graces of the imagination.

There is much in common between this and Leigh Hunt's emphasis on the 'ornamental part of utility', which he had hoped to cultivate in *Leigh Hunt's London Journal*. Dickens planned that poetry and fiction should regularly appear in *Household Words*, and a consistent attempt was made to treat scientific subjects in particular in an attractive way, by the introduction of dialogue, illustrative anecdotes, allegory, and similar devices. Information about Australia—for encouragement of emigration was an important part of the early policy of the periodical, during the years when Dickens was most interested in the work of the Family Colonization Loan Society—is often conveyed through the letters and narratives of successful settlers. These were provided by Mrs. Chisholm herself. Other writers tried hard to make the facts about topics like the postal system, the London water supply, or methods of marketing meat easily comprehensible by readers unaccustomed to making any intellectual effort.

What is still more attractive in *Household Words* is the first-hand and detailed knowledge displayed in its articles. The popular theatre, a visit to a workhouse or industrial school, the misery caused among the poor by a hard winter, an indictment of factory owners who refuse to fence in their machinery, a discussion of the legal disabilities of married women or of the law of divorce, are typical subjects. The writers seem really to know what they are talking about. This is true even when, as in the case of Dickens's attack on Millais' 'Holy Family',[1] we find the tone of an article or the conclusions reached distasteful or mistaken. There is no doubt in our minds that Dickens had actually seen the picture he was writing about.

The same quality of immediacy characterizes most of the fiction. We expect to find invention and verisimilitude in the works of Dickens and Mrs. Gaskell, when they appear in the pages of *Household Words*, but it is not confined to them. The

---

[1] *Household Words*, i (June 15, 1850), *New Lamps for Old Ones*, 265.

stories are independent of the rigid literary conventions which give such dreary monotony to Salisbury Square fiction or to the works of Reynolds in his later years. They have a closeness to reality which does not imply a narrow range of plots or the perpetual harping on a note of social criticism. There are legends, historical tales, stories of love and adventure, as well as sober narratives of lower- and middle-class life. A common element is their style. Command of the vernacular leads to ease in narrative and natural, animated dialogue. The absurdities of exaggerated sensibility are avoided, and characterization, while as a rule neither subtle nor strikingly original, has life and vigour. Of course there is much that is second rate, like the short serial *Mother and Step-Mother*,[1] which deals with a woman whose jealousy of her stepson drives her to try to murder him, with the result that her own son drinks the poison and is killed. Such stories, well constructed and competently told, nevertheless bring no poignancy or sensitiveness to the relation of tragic events, and are only a higher type of the sensationalism that finds another expression in the penny dreadful. But at the other end of the scale we find stories like *The Home of Woodruffe the Gardener*,[2] a most interesting piece of genre writing. The Woodruffes get their living by market gardening. They move to a new district, where lack of drainage causes cultivation to be difficult and unprofitable and is responsible for serious illness in the members of the family. In the end the land is drained and they achieve prosperity, though not before the old father has become permanently crippled by rheumatism and the son-in-law has met his death. Here is the drama of common life, told with detailed knowledge of how the poor live and suffer and work. It was not in the tradition of *Household Words* to leave it as a tragedy; for tragedy is still regarded as lying in major and striking misfortune, rather than in the slow failures and disappointments of daily life. But all the

---

[1] *Household Words*, xi (May 12, 19 and 26, 1855). The story is by Miss King. (This and other attributions of stories from *Household Words* are derived from the copy of the contributors' book, now at the Dickens House, 48 Doughty Street.)

[2] Ibid. i (August 24 to September 7, 1850), by Harriet Martineau.

same, such stories bring technical competence to describing the
solid realities of human toil and effort, sorrow and joy. This
being so, the fiction in *Household Words* has recognizable affinities
with some of the world's great literature—a thing which can be
said of few cheap or expensive periodicals, now or in its own day.

John Cassell showed his interest in the education of the lower
orders as early as 1850, when he published *The Literature of
Working Men*. The contributors were all labourers and tradesmen.
At the end of 1853 he started his *Illustrated Family Paper;* his
motives in doing so are well described by his biographer, G.
Holden Pike:

> It was an age in which sensational stories of an immoral tendency
> were largely sold in weekly numbers; but probably still more mis-
> chief was done by the more ample broadsides of certain periodicals
> which pandered to low or even criminal tastes. John Cassell saw all
> of these evils and deplored them as seriously as anyone. His desire
> was naturally to provide something by way of counteraction.

His *Family Paper* reflected this desire; it reflects also the character
of its founder, a self-made man, a teetotaller, one who rose early
and broke the ice on his bath on winter mornings. For some years
its contents consisted of about a third fiction, the rest being
biography, history, current affairs and so on. The fiction was of
a strenuous kind. Adventure as a theme prevailed over romance
—typical titles are *The Arctic Crusoe, Joel Kirkham's First Experience of the American Backwoods, Black Thursday—the Great Bush
Fire of Victoria*. This is very like the fiction that was published in
religious periodicals such as the *Leisure Hour*, and will be discussed
in the next chapter. Many stories and articles advocate total
abstention from alcohol. The moderate drinker is a particular
object of attack. The ethics of cheerfulness, content, industry,
thrift and charity are vigorously advocated. Criticism of the
established order is avoided, and all the emphasis is laid on the
necessity of reforming not institutions but individuals.

In 1857, apparently after Cassell had become involved in considerable financial difficulties, the *Family Paper* became the property of himself conjointly with his partners, Petter and Galpin,

and was changed in size from eight large to sixteen smaller but still sizeable pages—further evidence of the popularity of periodicals of that size. The proportion of fiction was increased, and romantic and sensational themes began to predominate. But the advocacy of temperance, frugality and self-help was maintained.

A final example of this kind of periodical is the *British Workman*, an illustrated monthly paper which began in 1855. It is wholeheartedly moral in purpose, and makes no attempt to give information on general topics. Fiction and non-fiction have a consistent message. They attack smoking, drinking, even snuff-taking; they are against strikes and Sunday excursions and the opening of public houses on the Sabbath; they preach the virtues of charity, thrift, prudence, perseverance, content, self-help, kindness to animals, and unexpectedly enlightened treatment of children. Adjurations to temperance and thrift tend to be accompanied by elaborate calculations of the money that can be saved by forsaking the opposite vices; there are even statistics of the amount of time consumed in snuff-taking by an addict. And, as in almost all the stories in periodicals of this type, virtue is rewarded, not only by the pleasures of an easy conscience, but also in a material way.

VII

'A PURIFIED PENNY PRESS'—II

THE periodicals considered in the last chapter were not published by any specific religious organization, nor were they directly devoted to propagating the views of any particular sect. The virtues that most of them emphasized were not, it is true, incompatible with the teachings of Christianity, but they were a very practical and limited interpretation of the Christian ethic. The motive which was to stimulate the poor to be clean, thrifty, industrious and so on was a very thinly disguised self-interest, and the reward of these virtues was tangible and immediate. Often, as in the following extract from the *British Workman*, prosperity was vaguely described as the work of God:

> His progress in the business was rapid, for he was a youth of quick parts, and of an enlightened understanding. His moral deportment was also uniformly consistent; and he found favour in the eyes of all with whom he had become acquainted. Thus the Lord smiled upon him! and as he continued to receive from his heavenly Father fresh manifestations of the Divine regard, his gratitude kept pace with his mercies, and his early piety began to assume a more healthy and elevated character.

But the successful apprentice of this story finds the manifestations of the divine regard in material prosperity. The general attitude in both fiction and non-fiction was this-worldly.

The opposite quality of other-worldliness would have been claimed for their publications by the organizations and individuals which between 1848 and 1854 established eight specifically religious cheap papers. Since it was the evangelicals who took the gravest view of popular literature, they were the most active in this field. Miss Fanny Mayne's *True Briton* first appeared in 1851, and in 1852 the Religious Tract Society began to publish the *Leisure Hour*. These were more subtle and less direct in their efforts to convert than were the *Churchman's Penny Magazine*, the *Mother's Friend*, the *Sunday at Home*, and the *Family Paper*, all of which used fiction in exactly the same way as a tract does. Against these six evangelical publications, some of which ran for many years, the High Church party set only the *Penny Post*, never widely circulated, and the S.P.C.K. publication, the *Home Friend*, which lasted only four years.

The proportion of fiction in all these was lower than in the more secular productions of the purified penny press, and of course much lower than in the widely circulated penny weeklies of the *Family Herald* type. But in many ways the *True Briton* and the *Leisure Hour* are much like *Cassell's Illustrated Family Paper*, being prepared to gild the pill of the full evangelical doctrine with a reasonable amount of artistry. They contain many articles, some of an instructive kind, others concerned with working-class conditions and claims. Both show real knowledge of the poor, and are at times remarkably liberal, as when the *True Briton* advocates early closing and the Saturday half-holiday, and even suggests that town and indoor workers should once a month, or once a quarter at least, have a holiday from Saturday till Monday, so that they can get to the country without travelling on Sunday. The *Leisure Hour* also could write strongly about sanitation and early closing, and both these papers express a deep and sensible interest in the problem of housing.

But the general attitude is that it is the responsibility of working-class people to help themselves. The undeserving poor, by thrift-lessness, drink, extravagance and dirt do far more to cause their misery than any employer or system. Emigration is encouraged, and those qualities of spunk and resolution praised which are supposed to lead to success.

It will at once be recognized that this is the same message as was being conveyed by the less specifically religious periodicals. The difference is that Miss Mayne and the Religious Tract Society see these qualities as the result of divine grace. This is most clearly stated in articles and editorials. The stories have the same message, but it does not obtrude itself too much, and many of them are good. This is particularly interesting in view of the somewhat limiting 'essential rules of healthful fiction' laid down by the Religious Tract Society.[1] These were that stories should be

1. *Moral*—no vice being invested with interest;
2. *Natural*—true both to nature and to fact, free from false representations of life and exaggerations of character;
3. *Unexciting*—leaving the spirit calm and the passions not unduly moved.

It may be that much of the world's great fiction fails to obey these rules, but in some ways they had a very good effect. Writers were forced to base their stories on life, and to choose subjects which have some intrinsic interest. Serials like *Slow Sam; or, the Orphan Family in London*,[2] though this particular example breaks out into sensationalism with a murder and false accusation at the end, give credible pictures of life as it must have been known to the readers. Sam and his sister care for the younger members of the family and struggle, not unsuccessfully, to establish a home and keep them all respectable. After a surfeit of heroines who, when reduced to poverty, have no resource but to be oppressed as governesses or poor relations, or, on a humbler plane, to starve to death while sewing shirts, what a pleasure to make the acquaintance of Rose Morton, a hard-working, sharp-tongued, good-hearted girl who keeps their miserable rooms clean and tidy, cooks the meals for the family, and earns money by sewing in her spare time. Similarly, the heroine of *Oriana; or, the Wreck in the Arctic Regions*, a good adventure story, endures shipwreck and the privations and exposure of an Arctic winter with efficiency, resource, cheerfulness, and never a faint. *Jane Rutherford; or, the Miner's Strike*, which is by Miss Mayne herself, makes the contrast articulate. The heroine has a tiff with her young man:

> Jane Rutherford, had she been a young lady of the modern class, when she came home after the scene we have described with William Norman, would have gone to her room, and looked at the setting

[1] *64th Annual Report of the Religious Tract Society*, 1863, p. 10.
[2] This and the next two serials discussed appeared in the *True Briton* in 1852 and 1853.

sun, and rising moon, and watched the stars peep out one by one, and all this time she would have cried, until her head ached and her eyes were swollen. . . . But Jane Rutherford was no maudlin sentimentalist, no pining, dreamy heroine of a fanciful romance. She first of all had to dispose of the work she had been to fetch, for Jane took in plain needle-work from the ladies in the neighbourhood, which she had the reputation of doing well and comparatively cheap. I do not mean, indeed, that she made shirts for three farthings apiece . . .; but she was paid a fair and honest price for her fair, honest labour, such as it suited the ladies to give, and Jane to receive as a welcome addition to the weekly store.

She then locks away her earnings, looks at the beef pudding baking in the oven, prepares vegetables, puts out her father's clean shoes and sets the table; one imagines her, on her father's return from work, sitting down to her meal with a very fair appetite.

But it is easy to understand why readers who had to cook the dinner and clean shoes every day were less attracted by this kind of fiction than by stories of 'haristocrats'. The *True Briton* failed, probably because it pleased nobody. Less dogmatically evangelical than periodicals like the *Sunday at Home*, it certainly offended some of the unco' guid, such as the correspondent who wrote: 'The chess problems, Sir, I give my unrestricted disapproval of, and I marvel that you should introduce such an incentive to gambling in your pages.' On the other hand, those who wanted marvellous tales must have found the fiction in the *True Briton* sad stuff indeed, and lacked any motive for buying it in preference to the *London Journal* or the *Family Herald*. And those who wanted outspoken and uncritical support of the working classes against the rich would not be satisfied by it either.

The *Leisure Hour* had a happier fate. Its mission as stated in the first number is interesting, and calculated to attract a wide public:

> Business is a sacred thing, something enjoined on us by Providence and bound up with our very existence; let it then be prosecuted with all the energy and singleness of purpose which success demands. Let there be no intermingling of work and play. Keep the head clear and the hand busy till the bell rings for repose. The day will soon run round, and if its duties have been well discharged, we shall enter with an approving conscience upon the enjoyments of the leisure hour.

These will include reading such as this periodical will hope to provide. It is hoped to avoid controversy, to utter sentiments 'such as would find an echo in every section of the christian church', and to stimulate readers to 'the attainment of every virtue which ought to elevate and gladden our English home'.

The *Leisure Hour* made a consistent effort in fiction and non-fiction alike to make the most of the excitements of travel, exploration, adventure, observation, and recollection of men and manners in other places and times. This shows considerable skill in finding acceptable ways of satisfying the human desire for release and escape, without violating the principles laid down by the Religious Tract Society. Few stories deal with romantic love, there is little exaggerated sensibility, the characters are never of high rank or foreign birth. The reader's interest is to be held by truthful or near-truthful narratives, dealing sometimes with voyage and discovery in distant parts of the world, at others with the lives of ordinary stay-at-home people.

As in the *True Briton*, the opposition to the ethics of most cheap periodical fiction is sometimes articulate. In a serial called *Struggles in Life*, the poverty-stricken hero knows that it is impossible for him to marry. Though much attracted by a certain girl, he avoids her, in order to prevent the formation of a deep attachment.

> Young as he was, we must do him the justice to say that he was above the silly notion so prevalent in our own as in former days, that the mere sight of a young lady on a few passing occasions is a sufficient ground for forming an attachment to her.

A short serial, *Wanted, A Governess*, gives a conventional enough picture of the sufferings of a governess, but ends with a suggestion that would never be made in connection with the genteel heroines of the *Family Herald:*

> Better and more honourable to be measuring out ribbon and weighing pins behind a counter, to be waiting on the whims of a gentlewoman, to be nurse to the sick, or housekeeper to the rich— than to run the risk of tampering with the mind and hearts of the young.

The attitudes expressed in the next group of periodicals, for example the *Mother's Friend* and the *Sunday at Home*, were far stricter and quite specifically religious. They used fiction wholly to illustrate the truths of religion. The emphasis is on conversion and death. Not the sanctifying of the world but the withdrawal from it is the duty of the Christian. Theatres, operas, dancing, card-playing, novel-reading and bad company are denounced. Family prayers, private prayer, Bible study and strict observance of the Sabbath are the Christian's chief duty. The modern reader is struck by the lack of interest in social obligations, both within and without the field of personal relationships, except in so far as they concern the duties of educating, warning, teaching and preaching. These are strenuously advocated.

Stories in the *Mother's Friend*, which is designed to aid and encourage 'those mothers who have little time to read and little money to spend on books', are typical of the simpler ones in such works. The periodical is meant for a very humble audience, and the frequent allusions to the deaths of children and mothers are perfectly appropriate. The death-rate of children, especially among the lower classes, was appallingly high at this date, and it was reasonable to feel that people should be prepared to face this fact.[1] A story like *Little Bright-eyed Tommy, the Sabbath-school Boy* may not accord with our notions of how to set about it, but may none the less have been more comforting than reflections based on more modern attitudes are likely to be. Little Tommy, having lived a blameless life for eight years, dies in the odour of sanctity:

> The hand of disease has stamped its impress on the face of the once beautiful boy, and the grave-robes are folded around the perfect little form so admired in life; but the bud of beauty is gone to bloom in a more congenial climate—it was not allowed to unfold here— perhaps our sin-stained country was too cold!

[1] It is awful to realize how a thoroughly well-intentioned little periodical like the *Mother's Friend* could contribute to the incidence of infant mortality. A letter addressed to a young woman, whose mother has died, leaving to this eldest daughter the care of the family, gives directions for feeding the two-months old baby. Its sole diet is to be stale bread soaked in boiling water, strained and sweetened, and not too much of that.

Some good children are allowed to live on, to teach their parents not to neglect their duties, like the odious boy who would not start to eat his dinner 'because papa has not said Amen'. Other children are not good, and meet with their deserts, like the wilful boy in *The Unhappy Mother and Her Ruined Son*, who broke the Sabbath by going swimming and was drowned, while his companion ran away to sea and died of yellow fever.

There is an engaging symmetry about this kind of thing which is preserved in the longer and more elaborate stories of the *Sunday at Home*. This periodical was published by the Religious Tract Society from 1854 onwards, to steer a middle course between wholly religious publications and those 'which, even where free from topics and sentiments positively corrupting and frivolous, were strictly secular in their contents and tone'. It was to be a publication 'at once cheap and artistically attractive, which should unite the charms of style to the grave verities of religious teaching'. It was in no sense to be a substitute for church-going, but it hoped to make the Sunday at home more attractive, and thus to contribute to the struggle, then to be renewed, against secularization of the Sabbath.

Here again the emphasis in every story is on conversion and its consequences. These may be prosperity in this world or early and blessed removal to another. The former is illustrated in a story called *Firmness of Religious Principles*, which begins as follows:

> Frank Edwards, a young married man, employed as a workman in an English manufactory, was converted. . . . The change was complete, and from being notoriously trifling and thoughtless, he became a proverb for cheerful gravity and serious deportment.

Ordered to work on the Sabbath, he refused, and lost his job. He and his family were reduced to direst poverty, and emigrated. In America he got a better job than his previous one, and became comparatively well-off, till the same thing happened again. But this time his action came under the notice of a sympathizer, who honoured him for his steadfastness and gave him still better employment. The story ends:

Here again our mechanic saw the hand of God. His decision had again brought him into trial, and God had come to his aid. The new situation for which he had just engaged was worth much more than the one he was to leave. God had kept his promise.

While conversion brings worldly prosperity, sinful action brings punishment here and now. *The Unequal Yoke* tells of a projected marriage between a 'Christian' girl and a wealthy and attractive but unconverted admirer. An older woman comments severely: 'Emily Burton, if she be a Christian, which I fondly hope she is, will have some bitter portion in her cup; it cannot be that a child of God should so far disobey His commands and remain unpunished.' Then follows a story describing a similar action, and the fearful sufferings that ensued.

But early death was to be preferred to a long and prosperous life. In a *Sister's Prayer Answered*, we have the story of a young woman called Ellen Vernon. Ellen is the light and life of her family, till she is converted. She then loses all her relish for gaiety. Persuaded by her sisters to attend a ball,

> she spent a miserable evening, and on her return said to one of her sisters, turning on her as she spoke a look which she can never forget, 'You must never ask me to go to a ball again; it is no place for me.'

Time passed, and Ellen increased in sanctity.

> 'Oh, Mary!' she sometimes said, with all the yearnings of a young convert, 'if I could but die!'
> 'Dearest Ellen!' her sister would answer, half alarmed, 'you should not say so; it is not right.'
> 'I mean if it would please the Lord to take me,' was the meek reply.

And Ellen is granted her wish, and dies very soon, very young. It is made clear that this is much the best thing that could happen to her.

While the two High Church periodicals had small circulations and little influence compared with those sponsored by people of evangelical views, whether Anglicans or nonconformists, they are worth some consideration for their reflection of different opinions. In evangelical papers the emphasis is on the individual, whether in his relations with God, where all depends on the personal experience of conversion, or in his relations with society, where success comes from his own efforts. But the High Church attitude reflects authoritarianism in religion and in social philosophy. Great emphasis is laid on the unquestioning acceptance by the young or ignorant of the pronouncements of the older and more learned person who appears in many of the stories as the interpreter of the will of God. Articles hammer home lessons of obedience, humility, contentment with one's lot and station, and reverence for one's betters. *Laissez-faire* economics are unswervingly supported. 'Nobody is compelled to accept whatever wages another chooses to give him, nor is anyone compelled to sell an article at any but his own price' is the burthen of an article 'On Wages' in the *Home Friend* for 1852. Trades unions are often attacked as being harmful and unnecessary in a society which should be united by the 'beautiful feeling which connects the superior with the inferior, and binds the interests and the pleasures of both into one'. Security of property and inheritance is vital to the general welfare, and the poor benefit from them as much as the rich. It is hard to decide whether ignorance or the deepest cynicism underlies the logic of the following statement, taken from another article in the same volume:

> The rich man, therefore, though he appears to have so much larger a share allotted to him, does not really consume it, but is only the channel through which it flows to others. And it is by this means much better distributed than it could have been otherwise.

Let the poor man make his bargain, thankfully accept his wages, obey his master and be contented with his lot, and squire and parson will help him out of any difficulties he may encounter. One very striking difference from evangelical periodicals will be noticed here; the continued insistence on a fairly rigid hierarchical order in society, as opposed to the suggestion that rising in the world was at once a sign and a reward of virtue.

Yet there is in some respects a very healthy tone in these periodicals. The fiction is realistic, unromantic and didactic. In

6

contrast to more evangelical teaching, its emphasis is on life rather than on death. There are instances of early piety terminating in an early grave, and there are some of the pale, pious, pulmonary characters of whom Thackeray once spoke, but they are kept more or less in their place. *All* characters are described as striving and sinning, some more and some less, with the possible exception of the priest, friend or guardian who advises the young pilgrim on his way. In this respect the stories are better than tales which tend to divide mankind into converted sheep and unconverted goats, with a great gulf set between. And the hallowing of the affections and occupations of ordinary life gives a livelier and healthier tone to a story than the drawing aside of the hem of the garment which is too often represented as virtue in the stories in the *Sunday at Home*. While there is much minute searching of conscience over the smallest lapses, many fearsome disasters resulting from small peccadillos, this moral stringency is at times relaxed in favour of the traditional jollity of old England, as when, in a footnote to an exhortation to temperance, it is suggested that working people, as a substitute for the public-house and beer-shop, should 'purchase a small barrel of good beer, and drink it at home with their families'.

By the middle fifties the uproar about the corrupting effects of popular literature was beginning to die down, and the voice of reason, or at least of reasonable sophistication, to make itself heard. The main points made in defence of popular literature were two—that the desire for exciting tales is universal, and that the particular way in which the poor were having their desire gratified was not after all so very bad. The first point is clearly made in an early number of an undistinguished weekly of the *Family Herald* type, the *Home Magazine*, which in an article entitled 'Reading for the Million' poured well deserved ridicule on tracts such as those against Sabbath breaking, which trace 'by a train of irresistible logic the ignominious end of the last executed murderer to the early indulgence in that heinous sin'. It is pointed out that even the Tract Society itself has been compelled to mix narrative and incident with theology. Working people in particular need fiction, since they lack the energy to struggle with other reading matter, and yet need more than most the pleasures of the imagination. The same article continues:

> The love of the marvellous, then, to which it is the vocation of the romance writer to minister, is deeply rooted in the heart of men; . . . the wiser course for those who seek to raise their fellow men is to recognize what they cannot alter, and endeavour to refine a taste characteristic of our race ever since the world began.

That was written in 1856. In 1855 was established the *Saturday Review*, which from its earliest days published occasional articles showing keen interest in and some knowledge of popular fiction. These, though often marred by an unattractive note of patronage or disdain, yet show powers of acute observation and generalization, and are seldom betrayed into righteous indignation.

The first of these articles, entitled 'Weekly Romance', appeared in 1856, and was typical of the general attitude of the paper. It was based on a perusal of the *Family Herald*, the *London Journal*, *Reynolds's Miscellany* and *Cassell's Illustrated Family Paper*, which were taken to exemplify a large class of cheap periodicals. The writer regards them as harmless. (It must be remembered that by this date Reynolds had passed beyond his 'voluptuous' period, which is a pity, because the attitude of a dispassionate critic towards, say, the first volumes of the *Mysteries of the Court of London* would be very interesting.) The article says that 'if these romances have one characteristic more striking than another, it is that of an exuberant propriety'. And again:

> These stories are not very much like real life, but they depart from it in a way that is not much to be regretted. Melodramas are not altogether unwholesome food for the half-educated mind. Hard and mechanical labour is an antidote strong enough to carry off most of the pernicious effects of fanciful exaggeration; and the worst fruit of reading these romances is probably a transient fit of unreal excitement and overwrought sympathy. It is evident that the stories are not written for a bad set of people; for they do not appeal to bad passions or pique morbid curiosity. And in this sphere of literature it is the readers who determine the spirit of the publication, and not the publication which creates the taste of readers.

This last point is very important. It was suggested in Chapter I that the final failure of works like the *Penny Magazine* was due to the failure to gauge public taste. People wanted fiction, and though for a while they accepted informative literature with some enthusiasm, the demand for marvellous stories soon created a supply. The immediate and continued success of the *Family Herald*, the *London Journal*, and *Reynolds's Miscellany* shows that they gave the people what they wanted.

The attempts of moral and religious reformers to replace these periodicals were in the nature of things unsuccessful. How could the taste that was satisfied by exciting stories set in distant times and places, and describing the experience of impossibly perfect or imperfect people, be fobbed off with the death-bed morality of the *Sunday at Home*, or the sober and enlightened realism of *Household Words?* It is true that some people as they grew older would doubtless graduate from one type of literature to another, but there is always a fresh supply of youthful readers. On the whole it seems likely that among periodicals that aimed at the reform of public taste the success of religious publications was due to the support of the converted, while such non-religious ones as survived did so by their appeal to an essentially middle-class public. (For one thing, they tended to be a little more expensive.) An unsophisticated public is not at the mercy of the decrees of literary fashion, and is not easily bullied into recognizing that there are things that ought to be read—that the quality of one's reading matter comes into the sphere of morality. Such people read for pleasure, and pay for what pleases them. And the *Saturday Review* is right in saying that in the mid-nineteenth century they were pleased by 'decency, propriety, and an established, though conventional, advocacy of justice and affection'.

In *Household Words* of the same year is a long article entitled 'The Unknown Public', based on a perusal of five penny periodicals. They are unnamed, but one of them can be almost certainly identified as the *Family Herald*. The most successful of them (surely the *London Journal*) is stated to claim a circulation of half a million, a claim which the writer (Wilkie Collins) believes.

Allowing as many more purchasers of the remaining four put together, and three readers to each copy, the result is a public of three million. This is the 'unknown public' of the article, which looks to the quantity rather than the quality of its reading matter, and reads for amusement. Wilkie Collins gives a fair description of the contents of journals like the *Family Herald* and *London Journal*. Apart from fiction, they consist of

> pickings from Punch and Plato; wood-engravings, representing notorious people and views of famous places, which strongly suggest that the original blocks have seen better days in other periodicals; modern and ancient anecdotes; short memoirs, scraps of poetry; choice morsels of general information; household receipts, riddles, and extracts from moral writers; all appear in the most orderly manner; arranged under separate heads, and cut up neatly into short paragraphs.

But the serials are their most prominent and characteristic feature, and the striking thing about the serials is their extreme sameness.

> Each part of each successive story settled down in turn, as I read it, to the same dead level of the smoothest and flattest conventionality. A combination of fierce melodrama and meek domestic sentiment; short dialogues and paragraphs on the French pattern, with moral English reflections of the sort that occur on the top lines of children's copy-books; incidents and characters taken from the old exhausted mines of the circulating library, and presented as complacently and confidently as if they were original ideas; descriptions and reflections for the beginning of the number, and a 'strong situation', dragged in by the neck and shoulders, for the end. . . . The one thing which it is possible to advance in their favour is that there is apparently no wickedness in them. There seems to be an intense in-dwelling respectability in their dullness. If they lead to no intellectual result, even of the humblest kind, they may have, at least, this negative advantage, that they can do no moral harm.

Wilkie Collins's criticism is therefore literary rather than moral. And he is full of hope for improvement:

> The largest audience for periodical literature, in this age of periodicals, must obey the universal law of progress, and must, sooner or later, learn to discriminate.

Whether or not we can feel that this pious hope has been fulfilled, it is a relief to find a change from the attitude of self-righteous moral condemnation. For however silly, sometimes even vicious, the penny periodicals of the mid-nineteenth century may have been, they must have brought a stirring of the imagination, a sense of release, to people whose lives were often more wretched than we can easily imagine.[1] There is something deeply repulsive in the priggish and self-righteous attacks made by their more privileged contemporaries on one of the few pleasures of the poor.

[1] In another *Household Words* article, this time by Dickens (*The Amusements of the People*, i (March 30, 1850), 13), we find the recognition of this need for release, put in strangely modern language. Popular plays are described as 'the most obvious, the least troublesome, and the most real, of all escapes out of the literal world'.

VIII

'THE LITERATURE OF THE RAIL'

THE history of the cheap publication of novels is so fully dealt with by Michael Sadleir in the second volume of his bibliographical study, *XIX Century Fiction*, and in his articles on Bentley's Standard Novel Series and on yellowbacks, that very little need be said about it here. He emphasizes the fact that in 1845 the regular form in which a novel first appeared was three volumes at a guinea and a half. A shorter book might be in two volumes, but as the standard price was half a guinea a volume new novels were always expensive. The only considerable issue of cheaper editions at that date was in Bentley's Standard Novel Series. Begun in 1831, it reached its hundredth volume by the end of 1846, concentrating by this time on reprints of contemporary best-sellers. But each volume at this date cost six shillings, and in that respect at least had little affinity with cheap reprints of fiction as they were shortly to be known.

In Ireland, however, first editions of such novels as were published there commonly appeared in single volumes of small duodecimo size, and it was a Belfast publishing firm called Simms and McIntyre which in 1846 began to publish the series called the Parlour Novelist. This consisted of only fourteen volumes, all reprints or translations, and sold for two shillings or two and sixpence each. A whole novel was published in one small volume at a fraction of the price charged for the same volume in its original three-volume form.

This venture was so successful that it was followed a year later, in 1847, by the Parlour Library. Novels in this series included a few first editions as well as reprints; they were similar in size and appearance to volumes in the earlier series; and they continued to appear till 1863, by which time two hundred and seventy-nine volumes had been issued.

The Parlour Library initiated a revolution in the publication of novels, similar to that which had occurred some years earlier with the establishment of the penny weekly journals like the *Family Herald*. The number and tastes of novel-readers had changed, and publishers began to cater for them along lines with which we are still familiar.

The success of the Parlour Library was so great that in 1849 began a still more enduring and numerous series, Routledge's Railway Library. The main difference between the two was that first editions appeared very rarely in the Railway Library, and it was devoted almost wholly to reprints. Generally speaking, less originality was shown in the choice of books for this series than for the Parlour Library, which duplicated far fewer of the titles which had already appeared in Bentley's Standard Novel Series. Altogether the Parlour Library seems to have been selected with greater taste and independence of judgment. But in appearance and price the two series were very similar. The vast majority of cheap novels published during the period covered by this survey belonged to one or other of them.

No attempt can be made here to describe the novels in the Parlour and Railway Libraries. That would be an immense task, involving almost a history of fiction during the first half of the nineteenth century. Apart from translations and books by American authors, about three hundred and forty novels were published in the two series from 1847 till 1860. They go back in date to the eighteenth century—*A Simple Story* appeared in the Parlour Library, for example—while others, like some of Carleton's novels, were first published in that series. They include *Pride and Prejudice*, along with novels by long forgotten writers like Emma Robinson and Thomas Miller, whose works were appearing in serial form in the penny periodicals. That is, they include some of the best English novels as well as some of the worst. A fair knowledge of these two cheap series and of cheap periodicals at this date implies an acquaintance with fiction at the most widely different levels.

As is usual with cheap series, a comparatively small number of authors of established popularity form the mainstay of the

Parlour and Railway Libraries. Over half the total number of English books thus issued represent the work of fifteen writers, whose individual contributions range from six to forty-seven novels each.[1] Nearly ninety other authors are represented, in many cases by a single book. Every type of novel which was popular at the time is included, with the exception of religious novels. History, adventure, romantic love, fashionable life and the condition of Ireland are the main themes treated.

The title of the Railway Library indicated the usual attitude to the publication of cheap novels in its early stages. They were bought at railway bookstalls and read on railway journeys. *Chambers' Journal* in 1845 had printed an article with the title *Railway Literature*, dealing with Bradshaws, blue books, and newspapers exclusively devoted to railway affairs. This shows that there was not yet a supply of literature specifically connected in people's minds with providing entertainment on a railway journey, and early more or less complimentary references to the Parlour Library in papers like the *Examiner*, *Spectator*, and *Athenaeum* never hint that this should be one of its great functions. But the establishment of the first railway bookstalls by W. H. Smith in 1849 created an unprecedented opportunity for the sale of cheap novels, and from 1851 onwards the phrase 'railway literature' or some variant of it was used to describe them.

As with cheap periodicals, the publication of cheap novels roused some hostility among the moralists and pedants. *The Times* in 1851 published an article called 'The Literature of the Rail', which, stating that the sale of bad literature on railway bookstalls had not yet been publicly mentioned and attacked, made a very spirited assault on certain unnamed booksellers, and on the Parlour Library in particular as one of their chief commodities.

[1] The reader may be interested to know the names of these writers and the number of novels each contributed to the two series between 1847 and 1860. They were W. H. Ainsworth (14), Jane Austen (6), E. Bulwer Lytton (19), W. Carleton (6), Mrs. Gore (10), James Grant (8), T. C. Grattan (8), Mrs. Grey (6), G. P. R. James (47), F. Marryat (15), Mrs. Marsh (16), W. H. Maxwell (7), Mayne Reid (6), Emma Robinson (6), and Mrs. Trollope (7). G. P. R. James was the writer of whom the *Edinburgh Review* said that he wrote novels 'as a hen lays eggs—nearly as rapidly and at as uniform intervals, and with quite as few of the throes of parturition' (*Edinburgh Review*, xcvii (April 1853), 382).

Describing the way in which longer railway journeys began to create a new demand for reading matter, the writer says:

> It was then that the *Parlour Library* was set on foot; immense numbers of this work were sold to travellers, and every addition to the stock was positively made on the assumption that persons of the better class who constitute the larger portion of railway readers, lose their accustomed taste the moment they enter the station and present themselves to the railway librarian.

This article was strongly supported by the *Englishwoman's Magazine*, which, it may be remembered, had attacked cheap periodicals. Shilling novels are those stated to be read by people a degree higher than the working classes, and it is hoped that great publishers will issue good and useful works at a rate as cheap as that at which the Parlour and Railway Libraries have been issued. Such works, if they are to appeal to readers, must be as lively and as cheap as 'the useless and pernicious works, which it is intended that they should displace. One shilling is the price for which every railway passenger expects to obtain his or her literary entertainment.' These strictures seem rather hard on the Parlour and Railway Libraries, but as they are mentioned by name in the article it seems clear that the description 'useless and pernicious works' is meant to apply to them.

The extreme rigour of these attacks was probably not typical of the views of cultivated people. Patronage or disdain was more likely than condemnation. Thus a half column in the *Athenaeum* of 1853 notices recent cheap issues of novels; it sees little that is positively bad mixed with the good and the indifferent, and predicts that the trash will soon disappear. Charles Knight in 1854 wrote of 'the Railway Libraries—by which generic term we mean single volumes, printed in small type on indifferent paper, and sold mostly at a shilling'; he regards the entertainment offered by the penny journal and shilling novel as frivolous but not debasing, as likely to enfeeble but not taint the intellect. The *Spectator*, reviewing the book in which Knight made these statements, argues that 'information or critical perception cannot be acquired by running through "amusing" books, or inflated, exciting, flashy novels, at a speed almost as rapid as the railway carriage in which the reader sits', but believes that the cheap reading of the day is much better than that of past years. An article in the *Saturday Review* of 1857 is based on facts supplied by the W. H. Smith bookstalls. The bulk of their sales is of novels at a shilling or one and sixpence, and the most popular authors are Lytton and Marryat. Then come G. P. R. James, James Grant, Miss Sinclair, Haliburton, Mrs. Trollope, Lever, Mrs. Gaskell, and Jane Austen. The sale of many worthless books is attributed to 'the scarlet-and-gold, the cream-coloured paper, and the ogling lady' on the cover. (By now the yellowback style was well established.) Whatever the cause, there is an enormous demand for the literature of mere amusement. The writer feels that such a deluge of *eau sucrée* must produce results, but is vague about what they can be.

It seems that fewer people were perturbed about cheap novels than about cheap periodicals. For after all, railway novels, if in a different guise, were for the most part the ordinary recreational reading of the middle and upper classes, and an attack on them was an attack on novel reading altogether. Everybody read novels, and the general attitude was that it was an undoubted but venial weakness, like eating too many sweets. The people who took the whole thing seriously were in the minority. Even Miss Yonge was prepared to make a joke about the literature of the rail. There is an amusing scene in *Heartsease*, which was first published in 1854, where the heroine is told by her husband that her desk has been knocked over and its contents disarranged during her illness. He teases her about the exposure of her secrets, like those of the heroine in 'a green railway novel' (the earliest binding of the Parlour and Railway Libraries) which his sister had made him read, and gives a racy account of the novel's highly coloured plot. The very title of Cuthbert Bede's *Shilling Book of Beauty* contains a reference to the price of the railway novel, while books by two of the writers he satirizes, Mrs. Gore and Mrs. Grey, appeared in both the Parlour and the Railway Libraries. The vices of the lower classes were one thing, and must be vigorously dealt with. The trifling but pleasant recreations of the middle and upper classes were regarded with a more lenient eye.

IX

THE HEROINE

WE must now consider the world that is presented to us in the cheap periodicals and railway fiction of the mid-nineteenth century. We shall consider the people who inhabited it, their relations with one another, the rules governing their conduct, their standards and beliefs, and the assumptions about human life and behaviour that determine these things.

Then as now, the most important character in the world of cheap fiction was the heroine. Her difficulties and triumphs, particularly the former, are the predominant central theme of novels and short stories. As one character says in *The Confessions of a Pretty Woman*,[1] 'You were certainly destined from your cradle, Evelina, to be a heroine; and no heroine can expect to pass through life without many sharp trials.'

In the vast majority of cases the heroine conforms to a type already well established in English literature by the beginning of the period under discussion. A good description of her is to be found in an article in *Household Words*:

> I love her blushing cheek, her gracefully rounded form, her chiselled nose, her slender waist, her luxuriant tresses which always escape from the fillet that binds them. Any man or woman who attempts, from a diseased craving after novelty, to cheat me out of one of her moonlight walks, one of her floods of tears, one of her kneeling entreaties to obdurate relatives, one of her rapturous sinkings on her lover's bosom, is a novelist whom I distrust and dislike.[2]

Richardson, the Minerva Press, Mrs. Radcliffe and the sentimental comedy had all helped to build up the tradition of what at times one is tempted to call the lovely imbecile. We are familiar

---

[1] By J. S. H. Pardoe.
[2] *Household Words*, xiv (December 6, 1856), *A Petition to the Novel-Writers*, 484. This article, by Wilkie Collins, was reprinted in *My Miscellanies*, 1863.

with her in the works of major novelists in the early Victorian period. In *Family Herald* and *Railway Library*, the rather limited possibilities of such a conception are thoroughly explored. Every conceivable variation of time and place and situation is introduced. And we are left with a staggering impression of uniformity. On one thing at least the vast majority of writers, and presumably of readers, agreed, on their notion of ideal womanhood.

First, the heroine must be very young, beautiful, and graceful. Youth as a necessary quality is not surprising, when we think of poor Anne Elliot faded and haggard at twenty-seven, and Lady Blessington describing herself as an old woman at forty-six. A heroine past the age of twenty-three is a rarity, past the age of thirty an impossibility. Normally she is under twenty-one. Beauty and grace are equally accepted as essential; the cinema preserves this aspect of the tradition to this day, though in magazine stories it is a little weakened. But it was of course the beauty of the day, with the moral qualities that it reflected, that was inseparable from the heroine. Consider the following passages, one from the *Library of Fiction and Family Story Teller* of 1837, one from the *Ladies Treasury* twenty years later:

> With what feelings did he contemplate the lovely form before him!—the graceful-falling shoulders!—the slender waist!—the full-curving sweep of the downward portion of the figure!—the ankle that seemed made for ornament rather than support! all set off by the effect of female drapery.

> What work of art is half so exquisite as that modest moss-rosebud beauty which we sometimes see in an English girl of seventeen, before passion has scorched one half-unfolded petal of the flower, and while her brightest moments spring from home affections and mental pleasures?

Here is suggested much more than a certain type of beauty. In contrast to her counterpart in the modern magazine, who must be healthy, if not hearty, the mid-nineteenth century heroine was always unathletic, while actual physical fragility often added to her attractions. Apparently healthy young women were represented as incapable of very ordinary physical exertion; for example, one of Mrs. Marsh's heroines at eighteen finds the weight of a baby in arms such that she cannot carry him without being twisted all awry, while when another heroine with her own hands makes up the fire in her mother's sick-room it is to the danger of her health. The coals are too heavy for her to lift, and she is reproached for not having summoned the faithful (and middle-aged) maidservant to do the task for her. However, Angela and Olivia were at least supposed to be young women of average physique; but we also encounter the girl who is actually ill, and preferred for that reason. A young man on a sea voyage makes the acquaintance of two sisters.

> Of course, Harley's immediate sympathies clustered more closely around the sick girl than her sister. The frail, delicate, dependent form—the pale, lily-like face on which already death had seemed to set his seal, yet stamped it so lightly that it was only as the impress of an angel's hand—the low, sad tones that sounded like the softest breezy murmur from aerial harps—all impressed themselves so deeply upon Harley's fancy, that he would have given his life to know that health would once again revisit that cheek.[1]

Such situations are by no means uncommon. And even heroines who are described as tall and solidly built are as easily overset by physical fatigue or mental strain as others who appear more frail. This weakness merely makes them more 'interesting'.

It is hardly necessary to say that the heroine speaks standard English, and belongs, with a very few exceptions, to the middle or upper classes. A few deviations from these rules are admitted. Decent working-class speech and station are possible if the story deals with Ireland or Scotland, while a good many of the Lloyd serials and penny dreadfuls have heroines who are said to be the daughters of very humble folk, sometimes even servants themselves. But these village maidens speak and act exactly like the vast majority of heroines, though curiously enough their lovers often express themselves in some kind of dialect.

It is equally essential that the heroine should be religious in a vague kind of way. Sometimes she is given to good works, but this is rarer than might be expected, considering how little she

[1] *The Home Magazine*, vii (December 2, 1859), 222.

seems to have to occupy her time. Another qualification for a regular heroine was that she should be an only child, often with but one surviving parent, surprisingly old and feeble. Or else she might be an orphan. An orphan makes good heroine material.

The heroine's physical weakness and dependence were the counterpart of equally essential qualities of character. Except by some American writers, whose stories appear pretty frequently in certain periodicals at this date, it was taken for granted that women were inferior to men in all really important mental and moral qualities, and that parents had a right to the absolute obedience of their unmarried daughters, if not always of their sons. The heroine therefore, being both young and a woman, had two possible sets of masters. Her primary obligation, established by the law of God or of nature, and fundamental to the social order, was submissiveness to authority. This was her duty and her joy. The point will be discussed more fully later, in connection with relations between men and women, and parents and children, but two quotations will illustrate it. Mrs. Crowe, a writer of very liberal views, an impassioned advocate of better education and opportunities for women, whose books show an unusual quality of worldly wisdom, writes in *Lily Dawson:*

> The true and noble woman disdains to rule, either as wife or mistress; she seeks a lord and not a slave. Her love must look ever upwards; and, except in the maternal relation, there can be no true love, from woman to man, that does not.

While in another book (*Marmaduke Wyvil*, by H. W. Herbert) two characters discuss the heroine as follows. One says: 'What she considered true, and judged right, that she would say, and would do, in despite of the whole world.' To which an older woman, whose opinion is vindicated throughout the story, replies: 'It is a fine character, truly, . . . though not a woman's character; at least, not what I think a woman's should be.'

Another aspect of the heroine's complete and willing dependence on her parents or husband is the attitude that it is wrong for her to have a secret. Her mother before marriage, her husband after it, should have her complete confidence. (Compare Jane Austen's insistence on the importance of 'candour'.) One reason why a married woman should not have a close female friend is the probability that such a friend, in becoming her confidante, would come between husband and wife, Every act and thought and feeling should be open as the day. In Theodore Hook's *Fathers and Sons*, when the heroine, in self-defence against the tyranny of her father and the espionage of his housekeeper, begins, not to tell lies, but to conceal some of the truth, moral degeneration at once sets in. Asked a question,

> she hesitated—doubted—considered. And here, reader, mark how sudden and how sad is the first inroad upon that purity of heart and thought which so unquestionably characterized poor Jane when we first met her—and how inconceivably rapid the falling off from the singlemindedness of innocence, for which she was so remarkable.

More generally, Mrs. Trollope regards such confidence as desirable within the whole family circle. In *The Vicar of Wrexhill*, lack of openness between Mrs. Mowbray and her grown-up children precipitated the tragedy; for, 'without this easy, natural spontaneous confidence, the family union is like a rope of sand, that will fall to pieces and disappear at the first touch of anything that can attract and draw off its loose and unbound particles'. Later she refers to what she calls 'the hateful mildew of mystery'.

To keep secrets indicates an unwomanly self-confidence, and invariably leads to disaster. But it was quite different for a man. Her father's or her husband's business was something of which the heroine remained completely and contentedly ignorant. Again and again total financial ruin overwhelms a gently nurtured woman and she is left penniless, without having had the faintest warning of such a possibility. Approving and semi-humorous references to women's incapacity for business are frequent (as are similar references to men's incapacity for domestic affairs, common devices in life and fiction for emphasizing the differences between the sexes). ' "James never speculates", Mrs. Jellicoe was always saying, although, to do her justice, she understood as little

about her husband's business as any wife ever did, and that is
saying a good deal.'[1]

It follows that when she is thrown on her own resources the
heroine usually fares rather badly. But though we may become
impatient with her as she droops and pines away in the effort to
earn her living, the passages that deal with this topic are among
the most interesting and convincing in this fiction. For here were
real hardships and genuine suffering. There was no need to awake
the reader's sympathies by implicating characters in a tragedy of
quivering nerves and wounded sensibilities, or far-fetched and
melodramatic disasters. Too often, governesses and sewing women
were truly miserable.

It was in accordance with facts that the heroine as a rule tried
to earn her living by becoming a governess, almost the only
profession open to respectable women. A good deal of sympathy
for governesses was flying about at this time, and this is reflected
in fiction. Not many suffered as much as Mrs. Brunton's Ellen (in
Discipline) who, after nursing her little charge through a fever,
caught it herself, and at the command of her jealous employer was
shut up in a madhouse. The real hardships of a governess's lot did
not demand such sensational treatment if they were to stir the
reader's pity. Cold, unprincipled, foolish or over-bearing employers, insolent servants, rude and ignorant children, combined
with low wages and long working hours, were the hazards that
might make her lot a wretched one.

But governesses were at least fed and housed by their employers
and kept from absolute destitution, while occasionally their own
acquirements or the goodness of their employers made their
positions agreeable enough. Women who tried to make a living
by sewing were less fortunate still. Innumerable stories recount
the miserable conditions and wages of girls working in dressmakers' establishments, or for slop-sellers or private employers.
The experiences of Kate Nickleby were fortunate compared both
with the reality and with the descriptions of it in the penny
periodicals. Reynolds was only one of a number of writers whose

[1] *Chambers' Journal*, xiii (3rd series, February 4, 1860), 65.

7

eloquence was aroused on behalf of seamstresses. And as well as
those that concentrated on the workers, there were many stories
to show the influence of thoughtless buyers and inconsiderate
employers in making things hard for sewing women. *Chambers'
Journal, Eliza Cook's Journal, The Leisure Hour, Cassell's Illustrated
Family Paper* and the *Home Friend* are among the more sober cheap
periodicals, and likely, one would think, to reflect the interests of
the employing class rather than the employed. But all of these (in
common with many others) attack the woman who tries to give
less than a fair price for work, or refuses to pay till long after it has
been delivered. Such women are represented as oppressing the
poor—which in many cases means our reduced but virtuous
heroine. It was no wonder that one mother was appalled at 'the
idea of her cherished, her superior, her noble-minded, noble-
looking daughter, possibly living by her own exertions'.[1]

It is extremely interesting that when in penny periodicals we
occasionally do find a heroine living by her own exertions and
getting along tolerably well, the story is almost invariably of
American origin. In England the heroine finds it almost impossible to achieve any kind of economic security. Fortunately, her
days as one of the world's workers are usually not prolonged.
Either death or matrimony removes her to a more fitting
sphere.

Another quality displayed by the true heroine is an extreme
sensibility. She is governed not by reason, but by emotion. It was
not at all necessary for her to be clever, or well-educated, though
there is less overt hostility to the clever woman than one might
expect to find in fiction at this date, and there are quite frequent
criticisms of female education. But even girls who are stated to
be both clever and well-educated show little evidence of their
advantages in added self-control, nor was it considered desirable
that they should do so. No woman could ever be as clever as a
clever man. What mattered was the feeling heart. The quintes-
sential heroine is the girl described in the *Family Herald:* 'For,
while the poetry of feeling was her element, Harriet was not an

[1] Lady Lyons, *Olivia*, 1848, p. 11.

intellectual person—she was more spiritual than intellectual—her heart supplied the place of a mind.'

This overwhelming importance of woman's emotions is another assumption which is taken so entirely for granted that, though occasionally stated, it does not need to be defended. 'Woman's whole life is one long history of the affections,' says Mrs Grey, repeating what is after all a very ancient belief. Bell in *The Ladder of Gold* argues that feminine emotionalism and irrationality are happy for men, since woman is strongest and most lovable when needing forgiveness :

> Assuredly it is a very happy thing for us that their sensations have such an ascendancy over their reason, and that the logic of cause and effect so rarely interferes with the gracious flexibility of their natures.

This note of condescension occurs very frequently, this indulgence extended to a being whose inferior intellectual and practical powers lead her continually into venial folly. For the folly is far outweighed by the warmth of her affections, and the grace of her person. Who would wish to change the pretty creatures? Certainly not those whose homes are lightened and enlivened by their frolics.

> 'Dear, holy, and heroic woman!' cries one writer, 'how frequently do we, who too often sneer at your harmless vanities and foibles, forget the light by which your love so often dispels the darkness of our affliction.'[1]

And, again from *The Ladder of Gold:*

> Stern and obdurate strength is not the finest characteristic of women; they are most strong and most lovable in their weakness. In this aspect we discern their humanity, which brings them nearer to our sympathies. Even their errors and failures add a grace to our devotion by leaving something for our magnanimity to forgive.

No bounds were set to the power of her emotions over the heroine. Typical is Louisa in one of Mrs. Marsh's *Tales of the Woods and Fields*, who was 'lovelier than Juliet—softer than Mrs. Haller—innocent as Perdita—more tender than Ophelia'. She

---

[1] W. Carleton, *The Black Prophet*, 1847, p. 210.

faints when the horses run away with the carriage, falls into a decline when crossed in love, and dies of a broken heart when the man for whom she had previously pined, having married her at last, neglects her. News of an even mildly exciting event had to be broken gently to the heroine if perfect prostration were to be avoided. Reunion after separation was almost always attended by distressing physical symptoms. A reverse of material fortune usually stimulated at least an attempt at fortitude, and during serious illness, whether her own or that of another, the heroine would bear up, often in a manner to cause universal admiration. But bereavement was the signal for the unrestrained indulgence of grief, often lasting years, if not terminated by insanity or death. Julia Wetheral in *The Manoeuvring Mother*,[1] most unhappily married, loses her husband while she is still very young. Yet her spirits never regain their tone. Cecil, in the book of that name,[2] has neglected a girl to whom he has previously paid marked attentions, and she has pined away and died. 'All human skill had been unavailing. She refused to be comforted—she disdained to live;—but expired in peace and charity with all men—a saint—a martyr!—'

It is not that such conduct is described as just an example of how people behaved (which of course it was not). It is regarded as meritorious. Comparisons are even made between those who show proper feeling and those whose collectedness and resilience in time of sorrow betray their inferior sensibility. In *Trevelyan*,[3] the hero's marriage is delayed by the serious illness of the bride's father. She recollects the necessity of making practical arrangements, such as postponing the festivities to be organized for the tenants. But 'there was something so dreadfully thoughtful and sensible, and so chillingly unsentimental in all this, that involuntarily Trevelyan let go the hand which he had still held in his'. Augusta's character is presented as unattractively as possible. Her fortitude is described as 'mere deficiency', as 'want of feeling exalted into self-command, and the absence of all interesting warmth of disposition miscalled superior sense and prudence!'

[1] By Lady Charlotte Bury.   [2] By Mrs. Gore.   [3] By Lady Scott.

Trevelyan, who has all the author's sympathy, is struck speechless and immobile in a crisis, and when afflicted by grief tends to closet himself in his room and to emerge only to stare into space, clutch people's hands, and cast as great a gloom as possible over all the other characters.

This convention is maintained in the most absurd situations. The author of *Martin Beck*, a story of emigrant life in Australia, is torn between telling the truth about colonial women, and having a heroine who conforms to generally accepted standards. Thus Marianne and Katherine Bracton have much to do in their farmhouse, and are entrusted with tasks like going to the local settlement to bail out the bullock-driver when he has been arrested for riotous behaviour. But one of them quarrels with her lover, and we find that she is a true heroine after all:

> The next instant there was a sharp convulsive struggle at her side, and with a sudden exclamation that was at once a shriek and a moan, her beloved friend, amidst all her roses and her loveliness, fell back pale as a corpse at her side.

The faint is not all:

> Paroxysm had followed paroxysm, till the feebleness of the system refused any longer to support the brain in the thought that generated the convulsive energy.

Marianne remained more or less an invalid for months. There is no real place for this kind of thing in the bush.

Connected with the extreme sensibility of the heroine was a tendency to physical cowardice. In moral dangers she was both brave and incorruptible, but it was perfectly reasonable for her to be overcome by actual or imagined physical danger. On the other hand, an occasional heroine showed great courage in emergencies, though tending to crumple once the crisis was past. Such was the girl in the *Family Herald* who, when menaced by housebreakers, seized a loaded gun from the wall, 'and placed her snow-white and taper finger on the trigger'.[1]

Then the heroine must be very very pure. On this point there is perfect unanimity. This was one reason why she must be so

---

[1] *Family Herald*, i (July 22, 1843), 162.

young, for purity was equated quite simply with ignorance and
inexperience. Popular fiction at this period had no place for the
mature or sophisticated woman. The following passage is quoted
at length because it is representative of so many:

> We can scarcely hope to describe adequately, the beauty, the
> gentleness, the earnest sweet simplicity of Matilda Rashleigh's
> character. She was one of those few beautiful beings who are only
> to be found in the middle classes of society in this country; and,
> somehow or another, are not to be found in any other country
> at all. . . .
> Matilda Rashleigh knew nothing of the world. Its cares, its
> blighting miseries, and its feverish short-lived joys were all unknown
> to her,—she lived in a world of her own—a world created by the
> purity and gentleness of her own heart—her ignorance was indeed
> bliss. . . . Dream on, we would say to such gentle, trusting hearts as
> Matilda Rashleigh's; may it be long ere you awaken to reality, when
> there is so much more joy in the unreal. . . .
> We have said that it is in the middle classes of England only in
> which the purest, gentlest beings are to be found,—those young
> creatures, whom we look at with wonder, and feel surprised by what
> magic they have been nurtured so long with such exquisite purity,
> and kept so far from the contaminating influence of the great world,
> the experience of which is a terror—the thorough knowledge of
> which, bitterness and remorse. . . .
> Far distant be the day when mock moralists or frantic philosophers
> succeed in blighting that first romance and beauty of existence which
> characterises the truly English girl.[1]

Now the appeal here is complex, since class and national prejudice are exploited. But the fundamental thing is Matilda's purity.
The point is sufficiently familiar to every reader of nineteenth-
century fiction, but a little more must be said of the general
assumption, not just that the heroine must be chaste, but that
chastity was the whole virtue of woman. A good illustration
comes from *Cassell's Illustrated Family Paper*, a penny periodical
appealing specifically to the more respectable members of the
working class, those who would find congenial its message of
thrift, temperance, industry and contentment. In a serial called

---

[1] *Lloyd's Penny Weekly Miscellany*, iii (1844), 530.

Left to Themselves, published in 1860, a virtuous maidservant discusses one who has fallen:

> 'I looks on all sich as the dirt beneath my feet,' she said, 'and don't want no talk about them sorts of characters! There's only two kinds of women (high or low), and that's those as respects themselves and those as doesn't. Those as does, I respects; those as doesn't, no one respects—and I despises.'

Oh, what a lesson to poor, fond, tempted girls! ... But Susan was right in one thing. There are differences in rank and station—there are fine ladies and poor, hard-working women—rich beauties in drawing-rooms, and poor beauties in back kitchens; but there is no real difference, after all, so great as that between the frail woman who has fallen, and the virtuous one whom no temptation could lead astray.

Corollaries of this central proposition are sometimes ludicrous, more often suggestive of grossly distorted moral standards. Ludicrous is the insistence, found especially in evangelical magazines for women, that to engage an unmarried mother as wet-nurse for your child was dreadfully dangerous. Chastity once surrendered, there was no guarantee of the existence of any right principle in a woman. Chastity preserved, however, outweighed the worst vices. So that a writer like William Carleton, some of whose stories of Irish life are both touching and powerful, could write of one of his characters that, 'though a hell-cat and a devil, when provoked', she was 'amidst all her hardened violence and general disregard of truth and honesty, a virtuous woman and a faithful wife'.[1] The significance of the passage lies in the use of the word 'virtuous'. Chastity outweighs avarice, envy and wrath. Even more dreadful in its implications is the relief with which Mrs. S. C. Hall's heroine Marian, in the book of that name, hears that she was abandoned as a baby not because she was illegitimate, but because of her mother's unscrupulous ambition and avarice. 'How fortunate I have been!' she cries at the moment of revelation. 'How wide God's mercy is! My own mother!—*my* honest mother!—your sin was of ambitious prompting, not the vile

---

[1] *The Emigrants of Ahadarra*, 1848, p. 184.

crime, which—but I said it could not be.' Unchastity is far worse than cold-hearted pride.

Since female chastity was regarded not just as a virtue but as virtue itself, it followed that loss of it, whether voluntary or not, was the worst disaster that could befall a woman. The phrase 'worse than death' was used in all seriousness, and no degree of repentance or suffering could restore the fallen woman in her own eyes or in those of society. So a woman who has run away from her husband with a lover is described as 'a thing infect, impure, no longer worthy even to touch that hand which once had seemed to grow to hers'.[1] Not even the fact that the sin is involuntary makes any difference. A woman innocently beguiled into a mock marriage (a common incident in periodical fiction) regards herself as hopelessly tainted, and tends to be similarly regarded by others. While one heroine, forcibly violated, says to her friend: 'Caroline, I am now a polluted creature, the victim of Devereux's depravity, the mother upon whom Albert, when he becomes a man, will look with contempt, unless the grave, before that time, should close on me.'[2] (It did close, and 'the once gay and beauteous Countess of Rochfort lay a breathless corpse upon the sunny shores of Italy'.)

Few authors failed to hunt down the fallen woman with remorseless tenacity. Exceptions were Reynolds, whose moral standards were peculiar, and writers like Mrs. Gaskell, Mrs. Crowe and Captain Marryat. But words of compassion and understanding like those spoken by the family doctor in *Midshipman Easy* about the girl who excused her illegitimate baby on the grounds that it was such a little one are seldom found, whether in good or bad fiction, at this time.

Just as generally assumed as the chastity of the heroine, if less explicitly so, is the idea that marriage is her destiny. This is made clear by the attitude of pity or scorn shown towards old maids. Those who are content to relinquish their hopes of a husband may be pitied—those who continue their efforts are laughed at. 'The

[1] Mrs. Marsh, *Two Old Men's Tales*, 1850, p. 260.
[2] *London Pioneer*, i (June 4, 1846), 87.

dreary state called in derision, single blessedness,' says a writer in
Household Words,[1] while in introducing as his heroine a brisk,
plump, charitable, cheerful old maid, a writer in *Chambers' Journal*
feels it necessary to point out that she is much closer to reality than
the customary acidulated spinster of fiction.[2] Heroines never make
old maids (except for Lily Dale). Sometimes of course they die.
The chance to meet eligible young men, however, is all that is
needed by any normal heroine to ensure her future happiness.
Readers and writers would be in full sympathy with the sentiment
expressed by one woman when in reduced circumstances:

> ' 'Tis a sad thought for my mother-heart, that while commonplace
> young ladies are making some important conquest, which may lead
> to the legitimate object of all female triumphs—a happy marriage—
> my beautiful Lucy is patiently enduring the waywardness of children
> and the insolence of their parents.' [3]

A very important rule of behaviour was that a woman did not
allow herself to love till she knew she was beloved. This was no
doubt connected with the general belief in the spiritualized sexual
organization of woman, in contrast to the earthy passions of men.
(Again Reynolds, specially in early volumes of the *Mysteries of
the Court of London*, is a rather staggering exception.)

One story refers to 'the deepest and heaviest burthen of a
woman's endurance—the degradation of having loved alone'.[4]
However, it was a degradation that a heroine had seldom to
undergo. The hero must often suffer the pangs of unrequited love,
but the heroine seldom failed to win all hearts.

It may be felt that this description of the heroine represents far
too consistent an attitude in the writers of popular fiction, that
the exceptions to all these assumptions about female virtue must
be so many as to invalidate any general conclusions. This is not
really so. Of course there are exceptions to most (though not all)
of the rules, even to one like the last. But the unanimity of opinion
on all important points is clear. Young and lovely, religious,

[1] *Household Words*, xi (May 12, 1855), 346.
[2] *Chambers' Journal*, xiii (3rd series, February 18, 1860), 105.
[3] *Ladies' Treasury*, i (1857), 100.
[4] Harriette Campbell, *The Only Daughter*, 1859, p. 100.

submissive and dependent, confiding and sensitive and chaste, accepting without question the destiny of marriage, the heroine emerges from the pages of the popular novels and periodicals as a well understood and consistent type. How far anyone believed that young women either were or ought to be exactly like her is another matter.

X

THE HERO

WHILE it is undeniable that nineteenth-century England was a man's world, popular fiction reveals a world of women. But though the heroine is much more important than the hero (except in stories of travel and adventure), the conception of the hero is in one respect more interesting. Instead of the tremendous impression of uniformity created by the female characters, we are aware of different and conflicting notions of ideal manhood, the impact of different literary conventions, and some faint approximation to the variety and inconsistency of human motive and character.

Youth, grace and beauty are traditionally less essential to the hero than to the heroine. While most heroes in these stories are young and handsome, and their appearance is often described in some detail, no great importance is attached to the matter. Indeed, like the heroine, if less frequently, the hero could be more 'interesting' for not being very robust. One very popular lady novelist describes her hero as 'a very interesting-looking person, very gentlemanlike in his appearance, being pale, but with a particularly refined cast of countenance, evidently suffering from ill-health'.[1] Not yet was bodily health regarded as a virtue.

The hero was most often a member of the middle or upper classes, with the conventional education, speech and background of his station. But writers like Prest and M. J. Rymer, and others of the Salisbury Square school, often chose people of respectable lower-middle or even working-class origin as their leading characters, and the men sometimes use a speech roughly indicative of their station. However, realism goes no further in the delineation of the working-class hero. The boy who by his own efforts

[1] Mrs. Marsh, in *The Wilmingtons*.

rises from the humblest position to one of great wealth and power will speak like an educated person from first to last.

Like the heroine, the hero is vaguely religious.

Submissiveness being the quality of the heroine, the hero is expected to be a dominant figure. But we do not often find him demanding the obedience of the heroine. In most cases it is freely given, since the readiness to obey is so essential to a true womanly nature. Where conflicts occur before marriage, they should end either with the graceful submission of the heroine, and with an acknowledgement that she has been wrong, or else with the termination of the engagement. No good can come of a marriage which is preluded by the tyranny of a woman over her betrothed. The doting lover, like poor Mr. Ellis in *The History of a Flirt*,[1] or the middle-aged and wealthy Mr. Addington in *The Bride Elect*,[2] who lets his betrothed trample on him, gets what he deserves when she throws him over. Similarly, as will be shown later on, the husband who fails to rule his household is not only miserable in himself but endangers the welfare of every member of the family. It is a man's duty to assert his authority, and if he fails to do so he is no hero.

It is much more difficult to trace any constant point of view in the matter of a young man's filial duty. The relations of parents and children will be more fully discussed in a later chapter, but it may be said here that most writers assume that a man has the right to choose his own wife, irrespective of the wishes of his parents, though there do occur cases in which superlative misery vindicates parental opinion. In the matter of choosing his career a man owes a certain duty to his father, but here again there is no one single consistent point of view. One would conclude from reading popular fiction that men differed in their opinions about the duty owed by a son to his parents—which corresponds to facts. Probably fiction tends to stress the obligation for dramatic effect.

When it comes to the matter of how the hero gets a living we find widely divergent attitudes, connected with conflicting ideals

[1] By Lady Charlotte Bury.
[2] By Mrs. Yorick Smythies.

of manhood. First we have the 'gentleman', a member of the upper or upper-middle class, who properly speaking does not have to get a living at all. He is of good if not noble birth, and possesses large estates on which he spends a varying amount of time. He is also familiar with the best society of London, and perhaps of Paris too. Frequently he is a Member of Parliament. His virtues are likely to be roughly proportionate to the amount of time he spends on the ancestral estates, engaged in their management and considering the needs of his tenants and work-people, with whom a true gentleman is always on excellent terms (for this fiction tends to preserve the traditional connection between virtue and rural surroundings). But since not all those who are born into good families have good estates, younger sons and younger sons of younger sons, like Cecil and Pelham, often live the life of the man about town. Their activities give rise to a good deal of headshaking on the part of fashionable novelists and their imitators. The best life is that of the country gentleman of good birth and fortune.

But it is very important to realize that the character of a country gentleman did not imply an overmastering interest in field sports. Quite the contrary. The fox-hunting squire appears chiefly as a target for ridicule. Lady Charlotte Bury was a writer of fashion-able and domestic novels who was intimately acquainted with the life of good society in the first half of the nineteenth century. In *The Manoeuvring Mother* she laughs gently at the handsome, worthy, faithful Tom Pysent, with his single-hearted devotion to horses and hounds. Much closer to her ideal of manhood are the studious Sir John Wetheral, the well-informed and retiring Mr. Boscawen, or Sir John Spottiswood, who writes poetry instead of hunting. Riding is properly a way of getting from one place to another, or a means of enjoying fresh air, healthy exercise and the beauties of nature. A true gentleman spends his time in the management of his estates, in the cultivation of his mind, and in the rational pleasures of social life. He is the hero of Jane Austen, sometimes appearing in a guise which she would have recognised, sometimes transformed to suit the tastes of the reader of penny periodicals.

Certain professions were traditionally regarded as suitable for the younger or poorer or more ardent members of the upper classes, notably the Church and the Army. But while many heroes of popular fiction were at some stage in their lives soldiers or sailors, the clergyman as hero is unexpectedly rare. A dislike and fear of sectarianism is probably one reason for the absence from the periodicals of characters in the tradition of Edmund Bertram or Henry Tilney or even Amos Barton. This is true even of the religious periodicals. And few novels in the Parlour and Railway Libraries reflect specific religious beliefs, though most of them are Christian in tone. It is possible that 'religious novels' were purposely excluded from the cheap reissues for fear of stirring up hostility. It follows that the curate as hero is not found in this fiction.

But many heroes were soldiers, with whom should be grouped sailors, like Marryat's Peter Simple and Midshipman Easy, and all the young men who set out from England to seek their fortunes in distant lands. Not all of them were gentlemen, but in their capacity as adventurers they tend to share the same qualities of courage, chivalry, generosity and resourcefulness. Note how the disreputable element in the picaresque novel has been suppressed. The hero tends to remain faithful to a single love, his difficulties to arise from circumstances rather than from his own folly and sin. This development is unfortunate. The hero as man of action is very dull. Marryat can sometimes succeed in stimulating interest and approval at the same time, as with the character of Peter Simple. But the interest, if any, belongs to the adventures rather than the adventurer in most such stories.

In contrast with many modern characters in fiction of the same type, these heroes get no pleasure from violence as such. Descriptions of fighting may be lively, and soldiers may be shown as in a sense enjoying the exercise of their skill. But the sorrow and waste of war is fully realized. The hero of *The Black Eagle ; or Ticonderoga*,[1] a story of pioneer life in Canada, is 'naturally gentle', though 'somewhat steeled by having to struggle and to act with

[1] By G. P. R. James.

cold and heartless men in scenes of peril and of strife'. This natural gentleness of the hero may be compared with the lack of interest in killing animals that has already been referred to. And the man of action is often still a cultivated gentleman.

A significant variation of the concept of hero as aristocrat and man of the world is to be found in Bulwer's *Lucretia*. The hero is named Percival St. John.

> He was more at home about horses and steeple-chases, than about opera-dancers, and beauties, and the small scandals of town. Talk on these latter topics did not seem to interest him; on the contrary, almost to pain. Shy and modest as a girl, he coloured or looked aside when his more hardened friends boasted of assignations and love-affairs. Spirited, gay, and manly enough in all really manly points, the virgin bloom of innocence was yet visible in his frank charming manner. And often, out of respect for his delicacy, some hearty son of pleasure stopped short in his narrative, or lost the point of his anecdote; and yet, so loveable was Percival in his good humour, his naiveté, his joyous entrance into innocent joy, that his companions were scarcely conscious of the *gêne* and restraint he imposed on them.

Here is Sir Galahad instead of Mr. Darcy. Religious and political ideas peculiar to the nineteenth century have shaped an ideal of manly virtue substantially different from that of the eighteenth. The contrast is pointed by a comparison between Percival St. John and Bulwer's earlier creation, Pelham. Pelham had ability, good principle and some seriousness of purpose, but all was disguised by an air of languid fashion. Shyness, modesty, delicacy, naiveté, even a spirited and manly gaiety, belong to the world of Miss Yonge, not to that of the dandies.

But this change in the delineation of the hero is seldom found in the fiction we are discussing. Popular literature is deeply conservative. The works of writers who were most influenced by the Oxford movement, or the ideas of Young England or the Christian Socialists, seldom appeared in cheap periodicals at this date, and were not included in the Parlour or Railway Libraries. Most authors stuck to the conception of the gentleman with which they were familiar.

But not all heroes belonged to the upper classes. The commercial middle classes are especially prominent in short stories in the periodicals, but plenty of novels deal with them too. The hero may be a struggling young lawyer or doctor, a superior clerk hoping to rise in his employer's business, the son of a merchant—even occasionally the son of a farmer or shop-keeper. In contrast to the heroine, he must succeed—how otherwise could he provide for her? Marrying a rich woman was strongly deprecated, unless the bridegroom was already so rich that his motives were above suspicion. Gentlemen usually preferred staying poor to trying to earn a living, but the middle-class hero worked. So must the poor boy who rises to wealth and position by his own efforts, which efforts are usually on the lines indicated in one story as follows:

> He had in his own self all the secrets of success. He was a very early riser. He never delegated to another anything which he knew he ought to do himself.
> He never procrastinated—never prevaricated.
> No pleasure had power to lure him from business.
> 'Business first and pleasure afterwards.' This was his motto.[1]

This down to earth morality is a long way from that of more aristocratic characters.

The social and economic position of the hero therefore varies a good deal, and roughly in accordance with facts. A problem is posed when we consider whether the same is true of the frequent instances of a masculine sensibility which is not so very much less exaggerated than that of the heroine. Tears, swoons, brain fever and decline follow any emotional crisis—and not only in the works of lady novelists either. Bulwer's Pelham, when Glanville ended the story of his past, 'burst into tears of gratitude and joy'. In *My Cousin Nicholas*, a novel by the author of the *Ingoldsby Legends*, the betrothed wife of a soldier dies suddenly. 'The shock was, under all the circumstances, too severe for human endurance; and, after a burst of irrepressible agony, he was borne from the apartment, insensible alike to the misery of those around him, and to his own.'

[1] *Cassell's Illustrated Family Newspaper*, vi (N.S., June 16, 1860), 34.

THE LEISURE HOUR

A FAMILY JOURNAL OF INSTRUCTION AND RECREATION.

No. 278.]　　　THURSDAY, APRIL 23, 1857　　　[Price 1d.

The Moonlight Conference.

Tears are one thing, though it is rather hard to suspend one's disbelief in a successful business man who, when his proposal of marriage was accepted, 'hastily took out his handkerchief, buried his face in it, and burst into tears'. But the young man who faints on hearing he has taken a first at Oxford is really too much. So is the middle-aged clergyman who succumbs to a prolonged fainting fit when his daughter questions him about a sorrowful love affair that had taken place fifteen years before. Many heroes showed ordinary fortitude, but no stigma attached to the free indulgence of emotion. As with women, if to a lesser extent, the signs of strong feeling claimed both sympathy and admiration.

Apart from this exaggerated sensibility, heroes in these stories are credible enough, and the picture of manly virtue presented is much more balanced than the picture of female virtue. Chastity takes its place as one among a number of good qualities, often taken for granted rather than enumerated. The hero will be chaste, just as he will be brave, courteous, kind, responsible and resolute. There is not the same determination to make him conform to a rigidly established pattern as is found in the case of the heroine. A final example will illustrate this variety, and be of interest to readers of *Guy Livingstone*. It is the description of the hero of a *Family Herald* story, with the title *William St. John; or, Modern Honour Exemplified. A tale of the nineteenth century.*

Above the common stature and proportioned according to the strictest rules of manly beauty, his sunburnt and unblushing front told of his indifference to sun or storm, and placed him undoubtedly above the butterfly lordlings and courtiers of the day; while his bright black eyes possessed equal power to charm or to intimidate. Those who would insult, or interfere with his chosen path, shrunk abashed before the proud fire that shone from his eye; but, in the drawing room, or the boudoir, whose eyes possessed more melting power, whose look more softness, whose glance more insinuation than his? His face of a faultiness [? faultless] and aristocratic contour was more enchanting for its constant change than for its inimitable perfection. His moustachoed lip expressed the most cutting contempt, or the sweetest smile—such smiles as few women could withstand; and if he laughed, he exhibited a set of white, regular teeth; but, to do him justice, he did not often bend his *hauteur* so far

8

as to condescend to such arts to attract the admiration he looked upon as his due. His black hair, luxuriant as a woman's, and dressed in a fashionable and becoming style, parted off a forehead that remained pure and white, despite of wind or rain. . . .

There is as much again of this, but enough has been quoted to give the reader a good idea of the character—and to allow the author to entangle herself in contradiction. This hero, as much as his namesake in *Lucretia*, looks forward to popular fiction of a new type, just as the gentlemanly heroes of most of the novels look back to the past.

XI

MEN AND WOMEN

THE most important common characteristic of indifferent fiction is that it concentrates on stock situations and relationships among characters and resolutely avoids most of the real problems of life. When it does tackle a real problem, it provides a facile solution, ignoring the fact that for many of our problems there is no solution at all. This is nowhere better exemplified than in the treatment of love and marriage in the popular fiction of the mid-nineteenth century.

We can forgive writers for overlooking the first real problem in the relations between men and women, which was the difficulty which young people must often have experienced in meeting members of the opposite sex. In the society of the time, girls were at the mercy of circumstances in this respect as in so many others, and their helplessness, the sheer inability to get to know eligible bachelors, must often have been the cause of great suffering. To a smaller extent young men were similarly handicapped. Such a situation now seems a suitable subject for fiction, but it is not surprising that writers fixed their eyes instead on the undoubted fact that somehow or other most young people did actually overcome this difficulty.

Once the first encounter is achieved, the writer must set obstacles in the way of lovers. A very high proportion of these obstacles exist in the circumstances rather than in the characters. Of these circumstances perhaps the most common is opposition on the part of the parents of either party, but more usually those of the lady. This is very serious, since unquestioning obedience was one of the salient qualifications of a heroine, nor would a woman who had a delicate sense of honour be a party to encouraging her lover to defy his parents. The steps by which such opposition is overcome are the main element in many plots, notably when the opposition is combined with a command that the wilful child should turn his or her affections in another direction.

The most convincing cases in which parental tyranny interferes with the course of love are those that occur in novels about Ireland, or in an occasional short story about thrifty lower-middle or working-class people. Some of Carleton's characters, like Fardarougha,[1] or old Burke and Cavanagh,[2] shrewd, semi-educated, saving, perhaps miserly, can be accepted as loving and despotic fathers. Their limited and unimaginative outlook is quite consistent with a sincere desire to do the best they can for their children. There is no real interest in the description of heartless and cold-blooded opposition to a child's reasonable affections. But one can feel some sympathy with the parent who genuinely wants the best for his child, though determined that the best shall consort with his own views. The submission of the child too becomes interesting when it is even in part a tribute to parental love, rather than a superstitious bowing before unreasoning tyranny, avarice or ambition.

Another bar to the smooth progress of love, and one often connected with parental opposition, is a reverse in fortune. Either the hero or the heroine is reduced from affluence to poverty. Instead of deciding that it is enough if one partner in a marriage is rich, the person who has been impoverished makes a noble gesture of renunciation and vanishes, to become a governess or to seek fortune, preferably in a foreign land.

Poverty on both sides is not often represented as a serious bar to marriage. True love is strong enough to overcome the dis-agreeableness of being poor. Anyway, some unexpected event, like the death of a wealthy relation or the patronage of another, usually intervenes to prevent the hardship from being too severe. Novelists often have things both ways, avoiding the real problem and giving the reader the satisfaction of knowing that hero and heroine are united by the most disinterested affection, yet ensured

[1] In *Fardarougha the Miser*.
[2] In *The Emigrants of Ahadarra*.

a comfortable existence. More rarely, the hero gets to work to improve his position, like Peter Simple, or Peisistratus Caxton, or Albert Smith's Jack Johnson.[1] Most unusual of all, and contrasting oddly with the exaggerated physical delicacy of her heroines, Mrs. Marsh sends Angela [2] and her husband off to India, as soon as they are married, to seek their fortunes together.

Real differences in station between lovers are strangely infrequent. Where they seem to occur, they are almost invariably resolved by the disclosure that the apparently inferior party is in fact of excellent family, but has been abandoned in infancy, or else exchanged for the offspring of a gipsy or nurse. Poor boys, however, do sometimes rise in the world and eventually win the hand of the master's daughter—a very ancient literary convention makes this possible. It is seldom achieved without some opposition, but fate usually gives the young man a chance to render his master some signal service and so soften his heart. But there is no corresponding device whereby a humbly-born heroine may rise in the world. She must be a lady from the start. Since a lady rarely sinks below the rank of governess, and since a governess is a lady still, it is not a genuine inferiority of class which separates a woman from her lover. To the high-born and haughty she may *seem* inferior, but they are not supported in that view. The daughter of a gentleman is fit to be the wife even of a man of noble birth, and opposition on the part of his relations is overcome once her real qualities are understood.

A situation which was probably a good deal nearer reality than those in which a poor girl makes a great match occurs in a serial in which the governess is wooed by the butler in the family where she works.

> 'Poor Malmsey', we are told, 'was very much in love, and Lucy, who knew she was born a gentlewoman, was a little ashamed that a butler should presume, as Malmsey evidently did, to think it no presumption in a man who had laid by five thousand pounds, and meant to keep a first-rate hotel in the west end, to aspire to the hand of a poor daily governess.' [3]

[1] In *The Adventures of Mr. Ledbury and his friend Jack Johnson.*
[2] In the novel of that name.   [3] *Ladies' Treasury*, i (1857), 163.

Here we have a situation full of interest, and a problem such as must often have occurred in the lives of the shabby genteel at that time. But as usual the author dodges, and Lucy is wooed by a suitor who is eligible for his personal attractions, his class and his wealth.

Traditional sources of difficulty for lovers are some kind of hereditary feud between their families, often based on religious and political differences. Popular fiction at this time frequently exploits the superficial possibilities of such situations, but has no notion of describing a serious and impassioned struggle between religious or political conviction on the one hand and romantic love on the other.

A major cause of trouble between lovers was the misunderstanding based on false information or mistaken suspicion. This ancient literary device was never very much good, and in a comparatively modern story written in prose tends to leave the reader longing to shake a little sense and frankness into the characters. One writer seems to feel dimly that it indicates a rather unlikely and discreditable lack of trust and candour between lovers, and attempts to defend it. Speaking of her hero, she says:

> Why was he so ready to believe ill of Isa? It is strange, but it is also true, that we are always most unjust to those we love best. We forgive many a treachery at the hands of those to whom we are indifferent; but at the least thought of change in a heart that *belongs to us*, that jealousy which is more 'cruel than the grave' springs up.[1]

Whether we accept this defence of it or not, it is a fact that the trick is frequently used.

It is the woman, as is traditional, who by some thoughtless or innocent act most frequently lays herself open to suspicion, or alternatively is the victim of scandalous or malicious talk designed to estrange her from the hero. A very satisfactory tangle can be created out of false information, mistaken conclusions, and a proud refusal to justify herself on the part of the heroine. Such incidents, like the other impediments to the smooth progress of a love affair already discussed, do not really assist in the

[1] *Reynolds's Miscellany*, xxiv (February 11, 1860), 98.

development of character. Both parties to a misunderstanding are represented as living up to the highest standards of conventional honour, and no slightest attempt is ordinarily made to analyse the rather discreditable basis of the suspicions they so readily feel.

All these more or less contrived and artificial obstacles to the progress of a love affair far outnumber the instances of what were surely, even a hundred years ago, more usual causes of lovers' quarrels. The existence or formation of another attachment, the discovery of hitherto unknown and uncongenial qualities in the beloved, the mere conviction that one has made a mistake, are all far less common than the most atrocious examples of paternal ferocity.

So far we have discussed the vicissitudes of courtship, its difficulties and dangers rather than its normal progress. It should be realized that to most of our writers the vicissitudes are the most fruitful elements in the relationship. The exploration by the characters of each other's minds, the patient analysis of feeling and desire as they are exhibited in very ordinary situations, would not be appreciated by readers of the *Family Herald*. The externals of courtship, the stolen glance, the blush, the hand held a little longer than necessary, the tendency on the hero's part to seek out the heroine on social occasions, the frequency with which he is able to perform some service for her—such are the episodes leading up to a declaration.

And a declaration once made and an engagement entered upon, it is still dealt with in this abstract and etherealized manner. No hint is given of the complexity of sexual love and the force of physical passion. Even in the comparative freedom of England lovers could expect little privacy, and this, as well as the moral code of the day, made the relationship between declared lovers very different from what we are familiar with in modern popular literature. 'They were affianced', says Mrs. Yorick Smythies in *A Warning to Wives*, 'and to Inez's delicate nature, that circumstance, instead of increasing her liberty of action, added to her coy and maidenly reserve'. And there is an interesting passage in

Bulwer's *Lucretia*, where Percival St. John is parting from his beloved for a few days:

> He rose, and with that loyal chivalry of love which felt respect the more for the careless guardianship to which his Helen was entrusted, he refrained from that parting kiss which their pure court-ship warranted—for which his lip yearned. But as he lingered, an irresistible impulse moved Helen's heart. Mechanically she opened her arms, and her head sunk upon his shoulder. In that embrace they remained some moments silent, and an angel might unreprovingly have heard their hearts beat through the stillness.

The significance of the word 'mechanically' is clear.

The limits of self-conscious daring in the description of the feelings aroused by love are reached in the *Englishwoman's Domestic Magazine* of 1860, which discusses the heroine's day-dreams as follows:

> There are many noodles abroad, of both sexes, and many hypo-crites and slanderers of human nature, who would call the child indelicate, and immodest, and I don't know what all, if for instance, I revealed that in one of these pictures Lotty beheld herself folded in the arms of a Man, and bending with him over a little fat face in a cradle. Well, I don't care, she did; and fifty other pictures, equally domestic, equally felicitous, equally indelicate.

Other aspects of this rarified treatment of love are the absence from novels and from most periodicals of the family joke about lovers and love-making—matters too sacred for jest—and the failure to use as a theme the love a very young man often feels for an older woman. Almost the only situation in which the real force of sexual passion seems to be indicated is seen as humorous, that is, in the picture of the husband-hunting spinster. Universal scorn is poured on this character, sometimes in very repulsive terms. She apes the appearance of younger women and adopts a variety of transparent devices to entrap her victim. Her motives are seldom analysed, for that might evoke sympathy, the last emotion that should be connected with her. In most cases it may be inferred that they are poverty, or the desire for a more honourable social position, the motives which alone are allowed to appear in descriptions of designing girls and their more designing mothers.

But sometimes the spinster is in love. Miss Barbara Jenkyns in *Petticoat Government*[1] has enough money and an assured social position, yet the main object of her life is to bring the unconscious Dr. Wroughtley to the point of a proposal. She is represented as being in love with him. The quality and force of her feeling are discussed very superficially, but its power is at least implied in the antics she performs. Mrs. Trollope wavers between compassion based on criticism of the accepted attitude in such a situation and joining in the hoots of laughter, with an unfortunate bias towards the latter. Most writers feel no impulse towards compassion at all.

Turning now from love before marriage to the relations between men and women within marriage, we find a contrast. The lives of married people are of course much less frequently used as a theme, the fortunes of young lovers being then as now more entertaining to most readers. But in so far as married people in these stories do more than provide a background for the activities of their children—the father, to oppress, the mother in whom to confide, and so on—their relations are described with greater attention to the interplay of character than to exciting events. This means that the comparatively few stories that deal with marriage as opposed to courtship make a more serious attack on real problems. Instead of concentrating on the external obstacles in the path of true love, they sometimes show the less attractive side of matrimony from the inside. The difference in outlook may be illustrated by two quotations. In the first, taken from the *Family Herald* of 1855, a lover speaks:

'Tell me, do you believe in the involuntary leap of heart to heart— the unwished-for attraction of one soul to another? . . . Oh!' he continued, 'it is a beautiful idea, that of the twin creation of the mind, severed at its birth, to wander perchance for ever alone, though, in some instances, to meet again and then to be united with bonds too strong for earthly power to break.'

Contrasted with this transcendentalism is the following passage from Lady Scott's *Trevelyan*:

[1] By Mrs. Trollope.

Marriage is a sort of moral microscope, the test of whose magnifying powers few characters can stand; and although it may sometimes bring to view charms of heart and mind, which the diffidence of youth had hitherto concealed; it oftener, alas! only exhibits in stronger lines the defects inherent in human nature.

As would be expected, most of the marriages that fail begin inauspiciously. The classic instance combines defiance of parental authority by the woman with mercenary motives in the man. (It must be realized that a runaway match could imply quite complicated villainy in the man.) While an elopement of a purely romantic kind might turn out well enough, the girl who disobeyed her parents in order to marry a fortune-hunter was in for a bad time. At best we shall find her sitting alone in her luxurious apartments, gazing dry-eyed at the hollow splendour that surrounds her, while her husband gambles away her fortune—at worst, she lies starving in a garret, attended only by a faithful retainer, her husband having fled to the Continent to escape his creditors. The characters of both parties are stereotyped, the woman gentle, affectionate, defenceless, conscience-stricken and clinging, the man good-looking and attractive, a skilled actor, impatient of restraint, unkind, and a spendthrift. Equally conventional is the process by which impatience on the one hand and anxiety to placate on the other become cold indifference and unrelieved misery. Very rarely does the woman who has summoned up the courage to elope show any disposition to stand up to the husband of her choice, and when she does, like Louisa in *The History of a Flirt*, her legal position makes effective resistance impossible.

At times, however, submission to parental influence could be as fatal to married happiness as defiance. In *The Young Husband* Mrs. Grey shows general misery to be caused by the fact that the hero is left a large income on condition that he marries the heroine, whose love he does not return. His mother persuades him to accept the legacy, and everyone concerned is as unhappy as possible. Another situation in which the social and mercenary ambitions of parents are condemned occurs when a mother, having educated her daughter for the purpose, more or less forces her into an ambitious marriage. But this latter case is not very much emphasized—perhaps it went a bit near the bone. However, it does occur, and such episodes provide the only instance in which this fiction even implies a criticism of the primary necessity of filial obedience.

In rare cases the ill success of a marriage is implicit in the characters of the people concerned, though their shortcomings may be less obvious than those already considered. These make the most interesting stories. There is a deadly sameness in the accounts of marriages that from the beginning are loveless on one side or the other, and therefore doomed. But a few writers seem to feel that there are greater possibilities in a relationship which develops. A husband's absorption in other pursuits, or his emotional dependence on his mother, a wife's growing determination to dominate, a husband's insane ambition, the formation of a new attachment, the undesired and unwelcome attentions paid to a wife by another man, plain incompatibility of temperament, even, in a less serious type of story, the urge to keep up with the Joneses —all these imply conflicts which are sufficient to engage the reader's imagination without straining his credulity or wearying him with contrived disasters.

If we consider now the presuppositions which underlie the picture of love and marriage presented in the popular novels and periodicals, the first is one that is observed with massive consistency in all English fiction at this date. This is the view that marriage is the most important event and the happiest state of life, and that most marriages are successful. Neither the occasional suggestion that, like most human institutions, it has its ups and downs, nor the descriptions of marital unhappiness just discussed make much impression compared with the fact that story after story ends up with the bad characters punished and the good ones rewarded, that the best reward is marriage, and that the people so paired off live happy ever after. This same fact that nine-tenths of the stories *end* in a wedding, to which most of the events described have been preliminary, gives the impression that marriage is of unrivalled importance. Though it is surely conceivable that other events and relationships should sometimes be equally decisive in determining the course or quality of a life— the choice of a profession, for example, the birth of children, the change from either poverty or wealth to the other extreme—the simple world revealed by this fiction has no place for such complications. Marriage is an end, a climax and a reward.

It is assumed that love will arise between people who are more or less of the same class, the woman at least being young and attractive, and that it will be independent, both before and after marriage, of physical compatibility, intellectual sympathy, and to some extent of material circumstances.

As is well known, the physical aspect of relations between the sexes is almost unanimously ignored in the literature of this period. The unimportance of intellectual sympathy is less invariably assumed (and is sometimes specifically denied), but it is implied by the conversation of lovers and married people. The arts, literature, politics, history—even religion—are seldom referred to. Politics in particular were supposed to be as far removed from a woman's interests as her husband's business, and, although 'accomplished', the heroine was not expected to understand the principles of music or painting. Even in religion an acquiescent rather than a crusading spirit was the ideal, except in certain specifically religious periodicals and novels. In *The Manoeuvring Mother* Lady Charlotte Bury describes a happy marriage. Isabel Boscawen is very young and silly, affectionate, domesticated, and a doting mother. Her husband is a middle-aged man, sensible, intelligent, with cultivated tastes. Their happiness is explained thus:

> It is temper which creates the bliss of home, or disturbs its comfort. It is not in the collision of intellect, that domestic peace loves to nestle. Her home is in the forbearing nature—in the yielding spirit —in the calm pleasures of a mild disposition, anxious to give and receive happiness. In the sweet humility of Isabel, and in the indul- gent forbearance of Boscawen, peace dwelt undisturbed by rival animosity.

The relationship of this couple was characterized by the main essential of a happy marriage—perfect submission and confidence

on the part of the wife. The love that united her to her husband
was essentially that of an inferior for a superior. When Isabel is
talking to another woman, Mr. Boscawen insists on joining in.
'My wife hears no conversation, Miss Wycherly, which her
husband may not share, I presume?' he asks; and again, 'Have the
kindness to admit me into the mystery: a wife should have no
secrets.' This attitude has the author's full approval. And the
theme of the whole book is the disasters that threaten a family
when the husband leaves the education and establishment of his
daughters in the hands of his wife, though he knows her to be a
foolish and wrong-headed woman, over whom he should assert
his authority.

This attitude is found at every level. There is the plain silly,
where a wife who demanded a fixed housekeeping allowance
'waived the sweet privilege of a wife's dependence, to accept the
uncontrolled salary of a hireling'.[1] There is the hortatory:

'On the breast of Lord Harrington you must repose all your future
hopes and wishes. From him there must be no secrets, no want of
confidence; to his better judgment leave every matter of importance.
In the marriage state, however well the parties may love each other,
discord will sometimes arise. Should such be your case, remember
it is the duty of the wife to yield.' [2]

There is the disillusioned:

'In all marriages, it strikes me that it is ten to one against *us!* If
I had a daughter, I should teach her this—that more than half of the
happiness of married life depends upon *us!* Whatever faults your
husband has, shut your eyes, for you will never, never cure them!' [3]

In *Valerie* Marryat expresses the view of an intelligent but not
very sensitive man:

'If ever there was a proof that woman was intended by the Creator
to be subject to man, it is, that once place power in the hands of
woman, and there is not one out of a hundred who will not abuse
it. . . . In a family, as in a State, there can be no divided rule—no
equality. One must be master, and no family is so badly managed,

[1] *Ainsworth's Magazine*, viii (1845), 526.
[2] *London Pioneer*, i (May 14, 1846), 37.
[3] Lady Scott, *The Hen-Pecked Husband*, 1853, p. 162.

or so badly brought up, as where the law of nature is reversed, and we contemplate that most despicable of all *lusi naturae*—a hen-pecked husband.'

And feminine submissiveness is surely indistinguishable from degradation in a novel called *Miriam May*.[1] Geoffrey May, son of a wealthy and despotic father, fearful of his father's opposition, marries his wife in secret, and for the same reason deserts her shortly before her baby is born, and returns to his home. For twenty-four years he makes no move to acknowledge her, though she is twice reduced to bitter poverty and is commonly believed to be a fallen woman. On the death of his father, he hastens to her side, and they are reunited. She exhibits nothing but joy at his return, and though the author shows a little disapproval he clearly thinks that he and Sir Geoffrey have made ample amends when Lady May's full rehabilitation is symbolized by her presentation at court.

The only circumstance in which the supremacy of the husband is allowed to be challenged and overthrown without the direst consequences occurs when the author wants to use the character of the dominant wife for the purposes of comedy. But nobody took this seriously as a description of marriage—particularly at a period when *Mrs. Caudle's Curtain Lectures* were regarded as the perfection of comic writing.[2] The characters in such stories were of lower-middle or working-class origin, where actual physical resistance and aggression on the part of the wife were not unthinkable; for example, in one story a hard-working wife locks out her lazy and errant husband, and when he comes home very late she pours water over him out of the window to sober him up. Eventually, she turns him into a worker. Such stories did not reflect the serious views of writers or readers.

Something of the beauty of an impersonal and serious common interest shared by husband and wife is shown in an occasional story which reflects a sober and intelligent religious belief, but such stories are very few. Since the souls of men and women are of equal value, heaven awaits them both. But here too the

[1] By Arthur Robins.   [2] They appeared in the *Family Herald* in 1845.

superior wisdom of the husband is asserted, as in Mary Brunton's *Discipline*, where the heroine at her marriage describes herself as

'a humbled creature, thankful to find, in his sound mind and steady principle, a support for her acknowledged weakness;—a traveller to a better country, pleased to meet a fellow-pilgrim, who, animating her diligence, and checking her wanderings, might soothe the toils of her journey, and rejoice with her for ever in its blessed termination.'

A conception of the relationship between men and women which excludes intellectual sympathy and regards it as essentially a union of superior with inferior is a pretty poor one. The popular fiction of this period gives not the most distant glimpse of the possibility, within marriage or without, of what Mill describes as 'complete unity and unanimity as to the great objects of life'. Apart from its poverty, this conception has another great weakness in that it excludes most of the real difficulties of the relationship, as well as some of its chief joys. Differences of class as a source of conflict are almost totally ignored. People who marry for love are traditionally poor, yet almost always the stories contrive a comfortable existence for them, pretending that the conflict between love and prudential considerations is not a real one. When any two ordinary people disagree about a course of action, there is a strong possibility that both are right or that both are wrong. But when husband and wife in these stories differ, the chances are ten to one that he is clearly right and she is wrong; thus the real problem of how such differences should be faced is dodged. Even when she is right, the good wife submits, the inference being that hard cases make bad law, and that far more harm would be done to the institution of marriage in general by countenancing a wife in disobeying her husband than could be compensated for by doing justice in a particular case.

Since community of intellectual interests between man and wife is specifically denied to be necessary, and even religious attitudes are mostly ignored, it follows that no conflict on these matters can arise. The possibility of a clash between impersonal objects and ideals on the one hand and private affections on the other is excluded. In spite of the influence parents exert over their children's marriages the influence is almost entirely mechanical, not overtly connected with the serious and fundamental differences in viewpoint between different generations. Hardly any reference is made to the conflict that may arise when a parent lives with a married son or daughter. The situation occurs often, and is represented as perfectly happy. Children as a possible source of trouble between married people are ignored. Yet some of our most serious moral problems arise from the conflict of duties to the different people who have claims on us.

The problem of ennui and satiety within marriage, the desire for something new, does not occur, except in the stereotyped figure of the fickle and worthless husband. It is never recognized as a difficulty that may be encountered by people of ordinary good-will. Equally overlooked is the fact that sexual passion commonly lasts beyond the age of, say, twenty-three in women and thirty-three in men.

Finally, and most astounding of all, considering the supremacy of the emotions as a basis for marriage, and the glorification of the state known as 'falling in love', this literature in effect denies the possibility of a conflict between love and the laws of society, and pretends that there is no real problem here either. Stories like *The Admiral's Daughter*[1] cheat. They invariably describe an irregular love affair as sheer misery. The actors are racked by remorse from first to last, and their relationship brings them no happiness at all. The reader is baffled by the problem of what can have induced them to fall in the first place. Physical passion and intellectual sympathy being ignored in connections outside marriage as much as within, no motive for flying in the face of society remains. Some mysterious and unspecified attraction, or else the workings of fate (that *asylum ignorantiae* of the novelist) must be invoked to explain why any character bothers to run away with someone else's wife, and this is not really very convincing. The writers are determined not to allow that there can ever be a true conflict between love and virtue, or between virtue

[1] By Mrs. Marsh.

and happiness. When there seems to be a conflict, the love is not true love, and the happiness vanishes before it can be enjoyed. The only writer to adopt an opposite point of view, G. W. M. Reynolds, maintained it for a comparatively short time. He pretty rapidly returned to the generally accepted attitude, and that in spite of the success of the *Mysteries of London* and the *Mysteries of the Court of London*. The conventions to be observed in describing men and women in love, irksome to great writers, were no less binding on the lesser ones.

The result of ignoring so many sources of both happiness and unhappiness in relations between men and women, is that popular fiction at this date gives a picture of love before and after marriage which is superficial and full of mistakes. It makes the following major assumptions: It is very easy to find and fall in love with the right partner in life, after which, a few external obstacles being overcome, there follows a marriage. Once you are married, only monstrous and misguided folly can induce you even to think of breaking your marriage vows. And if you do flout the laws of society, you will be miserable ever after. None of which can be called either convincing or adequate.

9

XII

PARENTS AND CHILDREN

THE second personal relationship which is very fully presented in cheap popular fiction is that of parents and children. But before approaching the topic of filial duty and the way it is treated, we must consider the conceptions of childhood and age in this literature.

In contrast to modern literature of a similar kind, there are no novels and serials, and comparatively few short stories, which take the experience of children as their theme. But even apart from such stories, references to children and childhood are naturally very common, and certain views emerge as pretty generally held.

The first point to be emphasized is that very few writers make any attempt to capture and describe the essential qualities of children. It is most exceptional for them to betray any genuine interest in them, much less any knowledge of their curious mental and emotional make-up. So what we get are frequent repetitions of a few stereotyped views, of varying usefulness to the writer.

The first of these, and the one of least value to writers and readers alike, is the commonly expressed belief in childhood as the happiest period of life. Such a generalization baffles comment.

Closely allied with it and very generally expressed is the second commonly held view of the child as naturally innocent, and gradually corrupted by the influence of the world.

> For the youthful mind is like a spring of water. How often should we not see that which was originally so clear and limpid, when first it issued from its mountain height, turning either into a troubled murky river or a madly overwhelming torrent? . . . Alas! for those streams and for those minds of which they are the types! How rarely do we find one wending its way through the perturbed scenes of life without becoming more or less deteriorated as it passes onwards![1]

---

[1] Lady Lyons, *Sir Philip Hetherington*, 1851, p. 38.

This attitude, which is intellectually more respectable than the belief in the supreme happiness of childhood, could have been used as a theme if writers had been sufficiently interested in the subject. The corruption—or education—of a child is a topic worthy of serious treatment. But it is touched on in a very superficial and casual sort of way.

These are theories *about* children. When we consider serious attempts to *portray* children, the vast majority of our writers show no sign that it has ever crossed their minds that children are in any important way different from adults. Here and there is a superficial touch, a reference to size or physical weakness, an attempt at childish speech, but that is the utmost concession to realism in the large majority of stories. One important reason for this— apart from the fact that it was much the easiest thing to do—is connected with the fact that a very high proportion of the stories about children either occur in the evangelical periodicals, or else are written from the evangelical point of view. Such periodicals were designed to attract young readers as well as adults; hence no doubt the use of this kind of subject. Now, since a child has a soul to be saved, and by the same means of conversion and grace as an adult, and since a very high degree of responsibility was assumed in quite young children, these stories tend to reflect experiences and attitudes which we (perhaps wrongly) find incredible. Children, like adults in the same kind of fiction, are represented as either good or bad. The bad ones meet with frightful experiences, which either kill or convert them, while the good ones tend to be unnaturally perfect, deeply religious, anxious to exhort and educate others, and given to dying in a very edifying way. They are capable of assuming and carrying out great responsibilities. Poor boys are prudent, thrifty, energetic, and conscientious in their efforts to rise in the world. And this kind of treatment is not confined to evangelical fiction, even if it is most marked there. It indicates a general lack of knowledge of children or interest in them. There is no attempt to convey their essential childishness.

A character very commonly found is the ministering child. It is not for the most part works of corporal mercy that occupy him, however, but exhortation and instruction, in which respect he is very like adults in the same kind of fiction. Harry, in one of Cassell's serials called *Left to Themselves*, is a good example. When befriended by a rich man and taken into his employ, he sets to work to reform the kitchen—and without any of the disastrous effects those experienced in kitchens might expect. 'Every evening', we are told, 'cook hastened to clean up, and tidy herself a bit, and with the other servants and Sim . . . to hear Harry read some very interesting tract or pious work.' Harry later taught cook to read, and persuaded the lady's maid

> to send to her poor widowed mother money she had been wont to squander on bugles, beads, artificial flowers, and other finery . . .; and he had induced her to practise writing and ciphering, and to give up reading dream-books, song books, and trashy novels, and study her Bible and other good books.

And such a child could teach us how to die. His parents both being recently dead, a boy of fifteen pines away, and expires with the following words on his lips:

> 'God bless you both!—I die so happily, you don't know! There's father beckoning me away! and mother and Willy and James [brothers who had died in their infancy] waiting with opened arms! Take me, father, for you always loved me well!—Good bye, all! Indeed, you must not weep; there's such glorious light where father is, and it reaches down to where I lay, and makes a golden ladder! And I die so happy, you don't know!' [1]

Perhaps this close connection with death is the thing that strikes us most of all in the discussion of children in this literature. The wisdom of the modern attitude of trying to protect children from any knowledge or death is debatable, if only because children invariably know so much more than we imagine concerning the subjects of which we would prefer them to be ignorant. But one cannot stifle an apprehension about the possible effect on a girl of not more than ten—her exact age is not given—of an experience like the following. Her mother, unhappily married for the second time, is dying, full of anxiety about the

---

[1] *Home Companion*, iii (N.S., December 29, 1855), 200.

future of the delicate baby she must leave to the care of an unsympathetic father.

It was a trying moment, however, to the mother; a trying moment, a terrible moment, when, one summer evening at dusk, she called the lttile girl to her sofa-side, and with careful preparation, led the way to the grievous announcement of her precarious state.[1] She then charges Selina never under any circumstances to allow herself to be separated from or to renounce the care of her baby brother. The little girl accepts the charge. The mother kisses the baby, leaving on his forehead a crimson stain which Selina wipes away 'with a handkerchief which she placed in her little swelling bosom, to be preserved as a sacred token for ever and ever'.

On the other hand, an occasional remark and an occasional story show real knowledge of children. To the belief in the natural innocence of childhood we may oppose remarks made by Mrs. Marsh and Mrs. Crowe. Mrs. Marsh takes the gentler view, when she speaks of 'the beauty, the charming society, the malice, the naiveté, the unexpected sayings and doings of an unspoiled and clever little child'.[2] The admirable Mrs. Crowe comments with calm insight on the miserable experiences of a small schoolgirl who is bullied by her fellows: 'Children, indeed, have little sympathy for each other; and are generally more like savage animals, whose instincts compel them to combine against the unfortunate members of their own community.'[3]

And, in contrast to unlikely stories of wicked or saintly children, we find a very occasional one describing the reticence of children, their irrational fears, their feelings of guilt over small peccadillos, the fact that they live in private worlds of which the most sympathetic adult has only a faint knowledge, worlds with values and standards utterly different from those of adults.

There are occasional comments on education in general scattered through this fiction—echoes of the useful knowledge controversy, attack and defence of the notion that education will really improve the condition of the poor, attacks on corporal punishment (which is almost always mentioned unfavourably),

[1] Mrs. Gore, *Self; or, The Narrow, Narrow World*, 1856, p. 206.
[2] *Tales of the Woods and Fields*, p. 63.   [3] *Linny Lockwood*, p. 70.

and even an isolated attempt to show the moralizing effect of beauty in daily life. But the points that are commonly raised are the badness of schools in general, the follies of female education, and the awfulness of a governess's life. This last point has already been discussed, but the first and second need some consideration.

Schools, whether for boys or girls, are represented as horrible places. Their defects are both moral and educational. The attack on boys' schools ranges from pious ejaculations, like 'Schools, those forcing houses of sin!' to more reasoned indictment, like Albert Smith's arraignment of his own school, Merchant Taylors, in *The Scattergood Family*. The points he makes are those generally raised by the more trustworthy writers—the tyranny of boys over boys, the contempt of 'every sacred feeling of home and affection', and the purely classical instruction. The defence of the public school made in *The Confessions of an Etonian*, by Rowcroft, does little to restore our confidence, since the writer admits all the charges, but justifies the system as toughening boys for the struggles of life. There are no indications in these stories of an acquaintance with the work of Arnold.

Girls' schools are, if possible, worse. 'Female schools are, in nine cases out of ten, public evils which ought to be put down by act of parliament, as injurious to the health, intellect, and morals of Englishwomen', wrote Mrs. S. C. Hall in *Marian*. Actual accounts of schools, as in *Linny Lockwood*, *Marian* and *Discipline*, show them as hotbeds of snobbery, favouritism, tale-telling, petty unkindness and ignorance. This belief lay behind the attitude of the father who determined for his motherless daughter that '*she* should at least escape the pollution of a school'. The result of this system is interesting:

> Evelyn Mervyn bore no evidence of any school. She knew what she needed to know, and she knew no more. An immodest word she had never heard, and if she owed that excessive ignorance to her home education, her girlish innocence, her faultless figure, and her lovely face found no sort of equal in any one of the many excellent schools that provided whatever you wanted at whatever figure you pleased.[2]

[1] A. Robins, *Miriam May*, 1860, p. 29.

Home education was the thing. In the case of boys, it was perhaps plausible to suggest that they would get a better education from a good tutor than at the average public school of the time. But it is hard to reconcile the clamour against girls' schools with the uniformly unfavourable picture of the privately educated pupils with whom the heroine in her capacity as governess has to wrestle. No school, one feels, could have made children worse than those Clara Scattergood had to deal with, and her case was typical. Another inconsistency lay in the fact that when we are given a glimpse of the heroine's own education we frequently find her in the care of an excellent governess who receives every consideration from her employers. One is left with the impression that the writers knew it was the right thing to be dissatisfied with the state of education, but were uncertain where the fault lay. Children are represented either as oppressors or as oppressed, either as monsters who delight in being as nasty as possible to their miserable governesses, or else as being bullied, scorned and corrupted at school. The same is true of teachers, who are either victims or tyrants. Perhaps the explanation lies in the fact that we are hearing echoes of various controversies that were arousing general interest at the time. Public school reform and the wrongs of governesses were being discussed, and so were the general deficiencies of female education. Writers with no particular interest and knowledge used these topical issues to lend vitality to their work.

The chief charge against the education of girls, repeated many times, was that it stressed accomplishments at the expense of useful knowledge, whether theoretical or practical. A 'well-educated' girl could sing, play the piano and harp, dance, draw, speak bad French, and make any number of more or less useless and ugly articles of 'fancy-work', and yet would know no history or geography or grammar, very little arithmetic or English literature, and be totally unable to cook a simple meal, make any kind of garment, or help effectively in the care of children or of the sick. While this was generally agreed to be a bad thing, few authors were prepared to create a heroine who was *not* able at least to play and sing. Still fewer, apart from American writers, let it be known that their heroines were genuinely proficient in the domestic arts. For, despite the attacks on the education of girls, most of this literature reflected the general demand for accomplishments in young women, and the general contempt of domestic work.

Thus we really have two inconsistent views of female education, often coexisting in the same story. It was generally agreed that heroines should be accomplished, and it was also felt that accomplishments were not enough. But it was the rarest thing for more than lip-service to be paid to the second of these views. Neither an ability to cook nor a knowledge of Latin exhibited the heroine at her best, and though she might occasionally be stated to have these powers, she was seldom shown exercising them. There is, however, only too much about her abilities in other directions, notably to sing.

But though there are so many references to the young and their education, these writers are not really interested in them as people. And the same is still more true of their attitude to the old. G. P. R. James in *The Forgery* makes it explicit in a few revealing words: 'Under any ordinary circumstances, the solitary meditations of a lady on the sear side of fifty can be of no great interest to the general reader.' The implications about what does interest the general reader are breath-taking—they are also consistent with the general tone of this literature. Love, adventure and intrigue are its main themes, and the chief characters are almost always young; love is as exclusively for them as are the active and often violent exploits of the heroes. Mrs. Thomson, in *Widows and Widowers*, says of the marriage of a man of sixty:

> O aged and reverend grandsires—or such as might be grandsires! leave to youth its amiable follies, its passions, its hopes! Time and nature warn us to live for others.

There is more truth in the following passage from *Trevelyan*, but its lesson is the same—the old must seek happiness in the lives of the young:

There is an awkward corner in human existence at which, bidding
of necessity a final adieu to youth, we naturally lose with it all lively
interest in our own prospects, and are therefore desolate indeed if
we cannot identify ourselves with the fate of others.

Old people—and old age began very early at this period—are
represented as living in the lives of the young, or as having power
over them. It is assumed that their private joys and sorrows, hopes
and fears are uninteresting. All the writer and reader care about
is the influence exerted by the old on the lives of the young.

The first thing to be recognized about this influence is that it is
one-sided. The relationship between old and young people—
which in effect means the relationship between parents and children—is one to which the subservience of one party to another is
as essential as it is to the relationship between husband and wife.
There are two moral principles which above all others are displayed in this literature. The first is that women must be chaste,
and this we have already discussed. The second is that children
must obey their parents. This obligation is, with one important
exception, completely binding, a kind of categorical imperative
which is never questioned. The fact that during the last hundred
years it has been largely overthrown must not blind us to the fact
that it is crucial for understanding and appreciating early Victorian
fiction.

The ostensible ground and justification of the parent's claim to
complete obedience was religious. Religion, as we shall see, was
fortified by superstition. The analogy between divine and parental
authority was made explicit, not just or even chiefly in religious
publications, but in the works of ordinary writers who might
have hesitated to repeat the religious argument, but were just as
insistent upon the moral duty it entailed. In favourable circumstances, mutual love and forbearance and the absence of conflicting
claims combine to give a highly idealized situation. Such a
relationship is described innumerable times. In a story from the
Family Herald of 1850, a son is commended for

the childlike warmth and perfect devotion of his filial love. His
mother was somewhat of an invalid, and he was always near her, to

read to her while she reclined on her couch, or to wrap her shawl carefully around her, and support her when she walked. . . . He united, in his manner towards her, the tenderness of a lover with the reverence of a son.

A later age cannot respond to the last sentence with the warm approval which the author clearly intended to evoke. Sometimes it is made clear that sons as well as daughters are under authority, as when Mrs. Grey describes one of her heroes as having been brought up 'under too strict a sense of subjection to paternal authority even to contemplate any longer so decided an act of disobedient defiance as a forbidden marriage must necessarily be'. As for daughters, their duty did not admit of a doubt. A dying mother's highest praise of her daughters is that

> 'Never, since they were capable of distinguishing right from wrong, have either of my dear ones given me cause for sorrow, or occasion for serious reproof. Whatever may have been their wishes upon any subject, mine have ever been paramount; nor can I remember a single instance in which their desires or feelings, however strong, were allowed to contend against mine.' [1]

Bulwer, in *Alice*, describes 'true maternal love' as 'the gushing fondness, the mysterious entering into every subtle thought and feeling', which characterizes the love of a good mother for a good daughter. To this the child should respond with perfect love and confidence.

The reader is attacked by doubts as to whether such an ideal relationship ever existed, and whether it is so very ideal after all. The modern attitude to the old is not very much to our credit, and there are no grounds for complacency in comparing it with the one most commonly described in this fiction. All the same, it is hard to maintain interest or credulity when we are confronted with innumerable wise and patient mothers, doting grandfathers, kind and generous aunts, uncles and guardians, between whom and the young people under their care the most unshadowed confidence and affection exist. One author does complain that 'the days of filial respect seem now pretty well gone'; and she

[1] *Cassell's Illustrated Family Paper*, ii (January 27, 1855), 26.

continues with a description of a state of affairs that sounds very modern indeed:

> Daughters answer their mothers, and sons argue with their fathers; we no longer tremble in the presence of our parents, or wait in humble patience till we obtain permission to sit down before them, but the son takes delight in talking the old man down, whilst the daughter shocks her mother's simple ear by sporting strange sentiments, and reading her lessons from a new work on worldly wisdom, published long since *her* less sophisticated time! [1]

We have all been treated to such homilies in our day, and doubtless there was occasion for them a century ago. But this fiction does not in general acknowledge the necessity. It does not admit the perennial problem that inspires such statements, the inevitable conflicts between people of different generations. As in the account it gives of the relationship between the sexes, the issue is dodged. What in the best circumstances is very difficult, the necessity for constant delicate readjustment in a relationship between persons who change and develop out of all knowledge during its course, is represented as being perfectly easy (or else disturbed by one stereotyped difficulty alone). Mutual devotion between parents and children, old and young, flourishes with hardly any evidence of the tensions that must sometimes arise in the trivial but important concerns of daily life, especially in an age when daughters, and often sons, lived at home till they married. Not only are trivial causes of strife left unmentioned, but so, except in the one matter of the choice of a husband or wife, are major issues. Everything that might make for real trouble is ignored.

Moreover, supposing such a relationship to have existed more or less as the books describe it, it may be very much doubted whether it was an ideal state of affairs at all. It exemplifies once more the stress laid in this literature on the personal life and the emotions. Parents and children are bound together by pure feeling, not by common interest in supra-personal objects, even of a humble kind. And there is something very repellent in the boa-constrictor concept of the mother, in the insistence on the

[1] Lady Scott, *The Hen-Pecked Husband*, p. 26.

complete confidence and complete submission of the daughter, the laudation of the mother's 'mysterious entering into every subtle thought and feeling' of her child. The poor girl not only had no private life, but would have been regarded as utterly depraved if she had wanted it. The dangers and disadvantages of such a relationship are apparent.

As well as the religious and fully rationalized basis for the relationship of superior to inferior between parent and child, there are many references to the irrational nature of the bond between them. As was suggested above, religion is fortified by superstition. According to this superstition, the link between parent and child had a mysterious power which operated even when the persons concerned were separated almost throughout the child's life. This link was far stronger and more instinctive than that created by fostering care and love. Repeatedly we are told that a child, nurtured with affection and kindness by foster-parents, is yet unable to feel for them as strongly as he should (even when the facts of the relationship are unknown to him), while, when the true parents appear, though still not recognized as such, 'a deep strange love' is spontaneously engendered.

But while fiction maintained that parents and children were joined in this deep semi-mystical union, and that daughters in particular owed absolute obedience to their parents, it also assumed the overmastering power of romantic love. Hence arose the moral conflict which it most commonly recognizes, and the one generally acknowledged exception to the rule of absolute filial obedience. The fact that our ideas about parental authority are totally different from those of the mid-nineteenth century must not make us think that the conflict existed only in fiction, or was unreal or absurd. It was just as real and serious as, for example, the conflict faced by a modern parent who feels seriously about his duty to his child, yet wants a divorce. This latter problem was as rare a hundred years ago and quite as unimaginable to the ordinary person as inflexible parental opposition to a reasonable marriage is today. As a subject for fiction it was traditional, but the tradition was based on reality. Where fiction and reality diverged was in the relative frequency with which the problem arose, and the extremely consistent solution reached.

After a long course of railway fiction and serials from the penny periodicals, one begins to feel that every second marriage in them is either being opposed by a cruel parent or forced on an unwilling child. The more submissive heroines bow to the inevitable with smug complacency, and unreasoning obedience is sometimes carried to pathological extremes. Filial duty is not a return for parental love and care. So one of Mrs. Gore's heroines says of her brother: 'Philip was not a spoiled child. But his parents did their duty by him, as they have done by us all. But even were it otherwise, is a child to *calculate* its filial duty as though the mere repayment of a debt?'[1] In other words, merely to be born creates an obligation.

The sanctions employed by parents to enforce their will were financial—the threat to disinherit; moral and religious—the appeal to the divinely ordered nature of filial duty; and magical. No other word describes the extraordinary horror attached to the possibility of a father's curse. It is very hard for us to accept this even as a fictitious possibility, at a period so close to our own day, but it meets us at every turn. Not just in the sensational-sentimental tales of the penny periodicals, either, but in novels by respectable writers. Reference has already been made to an episode in *The History of a Flirt*, where a father uses the threat of his curse to enforce his will on his daughter. A still more remarkable instance occurs in *The Ladder of Gold*,[2] a book which in general gives a sober and realistic picture of life. During the interview in which her father is insisting that she marry a man she does not love, Margaret kneels to him, but he remains obdurate. The lover she prefers resorts to subterfuge, and sends her a letter through her sister Clara. But the father discovers this, and Clara, a girl of much more spirit than Margaret, is so terrified by the threat of his curse that she swears to conceal the letter. This is in spite of the deep affection that exists between the sisters. And amid the deliberate realism of Miss Mayne's *True Briton*, when her father threatens to

[1] *Self; or, The Narrow, Narrow, World*, p. 75.   [2] By R. Bell.

curse Jane Rutherford if she marries a very deserving man whom
he happens to dislike, Jane is disturbed. While she reflects that
'the curse causeless shall not fall', yet 'a parent's blessing and a
parent's curse involve solemn consequences. They sow for a
future harvest of joy or sorrow—in which both parties share.' She
is prepared to insist on marrying William Norman, but not
without deep misgivings.

The novelist's consistent solution of this moral problem is
simple. Here, and here alone, may a parent be disobeyed. A child
has the right to refuse an uncongenial partner, but no right to
insist on marrying the person of his (or more commonly her)
choice. When this position is gently but resolutely maintained,
the cruel parent is almost invariably reconciled in the end. The
rejected one is proved to be of excellent birth, or receives a sudden
accession of fortune, or is cleared of scandalous imputations, or
performs some signal service to the father of the beloved, or is
vindicated in some other way. Occasionally, though one feels this
to be too drastic, the parent dies—leaving the too conscientious
child to grapple with the problem of reconciling common sense
with loyalty to the departed. But when the child submits to the
parent's dictation and makes a loveless marriage, unhappiness is
almost as certain as when the parent is defied and a marriage takes
place without his consent. It is assumed that the obligation to
obey your parents is exactly balanced by the obligation to marry
only where you love, and that happiness is possible only when
both obligations are fulfilled.

Here again we see the essential weakness of this fiction. The
solution of a serious moral difficulty is seldom so simple. Occasionally some unexpected chance does arise to make things easy
for us, but as a rule we have to be content with making the best
of a bad job. Conflicting duties continue to conflict, and we have
to weigh them against each other, hoping to achieve a reasonably
satisfactory compromise. On the other hand, we find that a duty
we have hitherto recognized can sometimes be flouted without
bringing misery in its train, and that it is possible to stifle conscience and get along pretty comfortably when we have done

something we believe to be wrong. It is hard to think that even a hundred years ago remorse was the unappeasable enemy it is represented to be in fiction. And while, to enjoy most fiction, it is necessary to accept the convention that the main characters at the end of the story will be either unnaturally happy or unnaturally the reverse, our credulity must not be strained too far. The causes of the happiness or unhappiness must be recognizable as such. We are too familiar with the incompatibility that so often exists between a person's relations on the one hand and his friends or sweetheart on the other, and with the frequent permanence of such dislike, to believe it can be so easily overcome as it is in these stories, even when the causes of the breach are financial or social rather than personal. Nor can we believe that to follow one's own inclinations is a sure road to misery. Most of us are pretty good at managing our consciences. On the other hand, a marriage that begins without passionate love between the parties can turn out well. But the assumptions underlying this literature do not allow for these possibilities, and altogether do not allow for the infinite variety and flexibility of human character.

It must be admitted that from time to time we come across hints of a more rational attitude. Periodicals like *Chambers' Journal*, *Eliza Cook's Journal*, and *Household Words* contain few stories of savage fathers. Filial piety is a duty, but only one duty among many, and not especially oppressive. In *Margaret Maitland*,[1] Grace Maitland, whose father has consistently neglected her all her life, sees no reason for devotion to him or deference to his wishes, and disobeys him with a clear conscience. The ill-success of Linny Lockwood's unhappy marriage is not presented as a punishment for running away, but just as what happens to a woman who marries a man like Vaughan Edmonstone. While in *The Vicar of Wrexhill*, when Mrs. Mowbray has fallen completely under the thumb of the odious Mr. Cartwright, Rosalind attempts to comfort Helen Mowbray in her perplexities about obeying her mother by saying, 'I hardly know how far a dutiful daughter may be permitted to act like a rational human being.' This only poses

---

[1] By Mrs. Oliphant.

the problem, and makes no attempt to solve it, but it at least admits the existence of a problem, and denies the possibility of an easy solution.

However, indications of this sort of attitude are very rare. The general conception is of a relationship between superior and inferior, in which right and power are all on the one side. Often mutual love softens the harshness of this idea, but veneration frequently becomes fear, and tenderness oppression. Yet, in spite of the well-established literary convention of the cruel father, there is never a suggestion that there is something fundamentally wrong with the whole notion of filial obedience, that power corrupts us all, and that Victorian parents as a race might have been better and nicer people for a little resolute opposition to their whims. So heavily are their claims emphasized that even a mild statement of the reciprocal duty to the child comes as a shock. Such a statement is the following, from Lover's *Handy Andy:*

> Sweet and holy is the duty of child to parent; but sacred also is the obligation of those who govern in so hallowed a position. Their rule should be guided by justice; they should pray for judgment in their mastery.

Yet even here, though by contrast the passage seems almost a spirited defence of the rights of the child, the relationship is envisaged as one of ruler and ruled. One can only wonder what dark reality underlies this ancient literary convention.

XIII

CLASS, WORK AND MONEY

THIS literature takes for granted the existence of a society marked by fairly rigid differences of class, differences based on birth and wealth. Most authors, including a high proportion of those who were writing for the cheapest periodicals, clearly believe that within this society the people whose lives are worth the attention of readers are members of the middle and upper classes.

To consider the first of these assumptions, we notice that in this fiction pride of birth is not very greatly stressed. On the whole it is true to say that wealth is what fixes the social position of the characters. There are few serious attacks on the *nouveau riche*, provided that he is rich enough. If he himself retains some traces of his lowly origin, his children will be indistinguishable from those of higher birth. Interesting evidence of the primacy of wealth in determining class is the fact, which has already been discussed, that men in these stories are often represented as rising from a lowly position to being able to aspire to marry well-born girls. But, since women could not make money, they could not rise in the world. Only the daughter of a gentleman was fit to marry a gentleman—or, of course, the daughter of a rich plebeian.

On the other hand, characters of aristocratic descent are represented as at least moderately rich, and as a rule wealthy. The very rich and the well-born tend to be identified as members of a single class—in *The Forgery* one of G. P. R. James's characters maintains, with the writer's evident approval, that 'it is by the frequent mingling of plebeian with patrician blood that the aristocracy of this country is so different from and so much superior to that of any other'. Little is made of the tragedy of impoverished nobility or of the comedy of the wealthy and emulous at this level.

Similarly, the middle class consists of people of moderate wealth, often but not necessarily of gentle birth, engaged in the

professions and in the less degrading forms of trade. Again, station
is determined less by birth than by money—the ability to live in
a certain kind of house, keep a certain number of servants, and
afford certain luxuries. But the suffering of impoverished gentility
and the comedy of the would-be genteel are fairly common
topics.

The lower orders, known to their champions as the industrious
classes, were quite simply the people who worked in shops and
factories and kitchens and gardens and farms, and could not speak
standard English.

The fact that individuals are frequently represented as falling
and rising in the world must not lead to the conclusion that class
distinctions were being obscured. People might be moving from
one class to another, but the classes were well defined (very much
as they are in English society to this day). In this connection, one
common misapprehension must be corrected. Popular fiction at
this date does not describe love affairs between dukes and kitchen-
maids. As has already been stated, difference of class between
lovers is almost ignored as a possible theme, and such startling
discrepancies are entirely unknown. A few stories describing an
alliance between a wealthy aristocrat and a poor girl—who is
always a lady—do use the phraseology which has led to this
mistake. In one, from the *Family Herald* of 1845, the accepted
suitor of Ebba, the daughter of a poor man, reveals himself as
'the Grand-Duke Frederick'. Ebba has misgivings about this
difference in rank, but he brushes them aside.

'Believe me, dearest,' he says, 'the nobility of the heart ranks high
above that of descent and high blood. The duke is not grand enough
to be worthy of thee. Of what worth is his long genealogy, his
unspotted pedigree, when compared to the treasury of thy pure
mind, the kingdom of love in thy heart!'

In another story, a governess describes a proposal:

'Yes, Lillian, gladly would I make you my own dear wife,' he
added, drawing me to his side. 'True, you have neither gold nor
station, but the wealth of a pure, glad young heart like yours, is all
I ask.' [1]

[1] *Family Herald*, xviii (May 19, 1860), 43.

But the social gulf between an aristocrat and the daughter of a gentleman, however poor, was in no way comparable to that between an aristocrat and a member of the working class. Certain people might rise, others could never do so. And those who rose identified themselves very quickly with the members of their new class, and helped to maintain its standards and taboos.

This does not mean that there were no attacks on certain social classes in this literature. The aristocracy, and individual aristocrats, were often assailed. From within and without, as leading a life of hollow pretension, as stupid, as dissolute and immoral, and as grinding the faces of the poor they were attacked. The first point was the stock in trade of fashionable novelists, and of the writers who used the same style in the periodicals. One of the most consistent attitudes expressed in these novels is that the life of fashionable society, though so exciting and interesting as to be worth writing about at great length, was yet utterly valueless.

Bulwer expresses this attitude in *Pelham*:

> The English of the fashionable world make business an enjoyment, and enjoyment a business; they are born without a smile; they rove about public places like so many easterly winds—cold, sharp, and cutting; or like a group of fogs on a frosty day, sent out of his hall by Boreas, for the express purpose of *looking black at one another*. . . . They are sometimes *polite*, but invariably *uncivil;* their warmth is always artificial—their cold never; they are stiff without dignity, and cringing without manners.

There are frequent similar tirades against the artificiality of upper- and upper-middle-class society.

The stupidity of the aristocracy is a point on which they are less frequently attacked. It is taken up by *Household Words*, and by a writer like Blanchard Jerrold, and reflects the attitude of liberal but not radical thinkers. A characteristic passage from *Household Words* describes certain lawyers as 'agents for half the aristocracy, who always run in crowds like sheep after the same wine-merchants, the same architects, the same horse-dealers, and the same law-agents'. The tone of this is one of contempt rather than of condemnation.

The immorality of the upper classes is more forcibly maintained by G. W. M. Reynolds. Even the royal family is attacked. There is a very amusing episode in the *Mysteries of London* describing the intrusion into Buckingham Palace of a sixteen-year old boy. (This of course was founded on fact.) The boy hides under sofas and listens to conversations between the Queen and Prince Albert—these are represented as quite colourless—and among the ladies of the court. Some well known scandals of earlier reigns are raked up, but much, much worse is hinted at than is actually said. ' "The events which have taken place in the family of George the Third would make your hair stand on end", replied the countess, sinking her voice almost to a whisper.'

In the attack on the aristocracy as heartlessly oppressing the poor, Reynolds is joined by a few other writers, who, however, tend to see the matter in a different light. He feels that 'the gorgeous robe and elegant dress of every high-born lady . . . is stained by the life-blood and infected by the pollution of the poor seamstresses who made them all',[1] and this whole story about the seamstress implies the individual depravity of all aristocrats (except the marquis who is the hero, and the illegitimate daughter of a duchess who is the heroine). But attacks by other writers, which are very few indeed considering the bulk of this literature and the audience at which it was aimed, tend to be directed against the prosperous in general, not just members of the upper classes, and to charge them with thoughtlessness and lack of consideration rather than actual wickedness. Women in particular are accused of trying to beat down dressmakers and seamstresses and deny them fair wages, and of failing to pay promptly for work done. Very rarely outside Reynolds is there a story showing a member of the middle and upper classes deliberately wronging his dependents or employees.

The most interesting thing about attacks on the morality and tyranny of aristocrats is that, with the possible exception of Reynolds, they are directed against individuals rather than classes. They never suggest that a radical change in the social order would

[1] *Reynolds's Miscellany*, iv (N.S., May 4, 1850), 228.

be a great improvement. Even Reynolds's writings are fundamentally, and perhaps deliberately, ambiguous on this point. His
early works and serials make it clear that he had republican
leanings, and that he would like to see a more egalitarian society
established in England. But his main characters are almost
invariably of good birth and some wealth, frequently rich and
aristocratic, and the good ones are usually rewarded by yet more
money and a higher social position. Thus, in the first volume of
the *Mysteries of London*, his heart is rent on behalf of 'the industrious many, by the sweat of whose brow the indolent few were
supplied with their silks, and their satins, and their velvets'. In
the second volume he prophesies that the poor will rise—the
tyrant will crouch at their feet—'as a mass ye shall triumph over
that proud oligarchy which now grinds you to the dust'. The
people will eventually assert the aristocracy of mind and virtue.
But not long after the second passage, we read that the hero,
having led an army against a usurping tyrant and reinstated his
future father-in-law as a reigning grand-duke in Italy, is himself
ennobled, marries the beauteous and high born Isabella, and
settles down to a steady and uninterrupted enjoyment of very
much more than his fair share of the good things of life. Reynolds
has it both ways. He appeals to his readers by his democratic
views, and also by offering them the pleasure of imaginative
participation in the life of a wholly undemocratic society.
According to his political and economic theories, members of the
upper classes were either fools or knaves, mostly the latter, and
used their power to appropriate to themselves an enormously
unfair share of the wealth produced by the industrious classes.
But in the pages of his stories, though these charges are frequently
repeated, such people are in fact represented as leading the good
life. Luxury, such as he teaches to be possible only through
injustice, is especially associated with his heroines. No blame is
attached to them for this—on the contrary, wealth and good
social position are the reward of virtue, to be apportioned to all
the good characters and taken from the bad ones at the end of the
story. The heroine of a serial in *Reynolds's Miscellany* called *The*

Slaves of England comes as near to being of working class station as any heroine of his. She is illegitimate, and earns her living as a needlewoman. Surely here was a chance for him to display his unorthodox social and economic views. Nothing of the kind. After incredible suffering, the wretched girl dies of a broken heart, rewarded only by heaven for her matchless virtues. Till we can estimate the comparative force of direct statement and unspoken implication, we can only guess which element in Reynolds's teaching would have more influence in forming the attitudes of his readers.

What to a modern reader seems one of the most cogent arguments against the existence of an aristocracy, the fact that a country cannot afford to support large numbers of people in great luxury and comparative idleness, is sometimes implied but not seriously worked out by Reynolds. Though he often said that he wanted to see a change in society, his attack on the existing order was really personal, and was directed against the wickedness of individuals rather than against the weak points of a system. In this respect, he does not appear in his fiction as a genuine radical, any more than the other writers who charged fine ladies with not paying their dressmakers' bills. An isolated example of an impersonal attack on the whole institution of aristocracy is found, most unexpectedly, in *Peter Simple*. Here Marryat writes:

> The law of primogeniture is beset with evils and injustice; yet, without it, the aristocracy of a country must sink into insignificance. It appears to me, that as long as the people of a country are content to support the younger sons of the nobility [presumably by giving them opportunities of preferment in church and state], it is well that the aristocracy should be held up as a third estate, and a link between the sovereign and the people; but that if the people are either too poor, or are unwilling to be so taxed, that they have a right to refuse taxation for such purposes, and to demand that the law of primogeniture should be abolished.

But such a statement conflicts both with Marryat's usual attitude and with the general viewpoint of this literature.

The fact that a great many people were expressing serious doubts about a social system which maintained such enormous extremes of poverty and wealth is revealed less by direct expression of such doubts than by the way in which writers *defend* the system. The defence takes several different lines. One is that God has made men unequal, and that differences in wealth and station are the divinely appointed consequence of this ordinance. Mrs. Trollope felt very strongly about this, and in *The Lottery of Marriage* she adds a note to some praise of Fourier expressed in the text, making it clear that he is not to be

> stigmatized as an advocate for the absurd doctrine of equality. There is great injustice in classing Fourier among the impious and crafty yet reckless preachers of this unchristian code; . . . an idea more pregnant with deadly social poison than any other which the heart of man has ever conceived.

A serial in the *True Briton* defends the existing system on the grounds of 'the distinction Providence ever has made, and ever will make, between the rich and the poor'; and a correspondent writing to the same journal speaks of 'the most distressing of evils —viz. the idea that all men are born equal'.[1]

Another ground of defence was that the operation of economic law and the general necessities of society demanded that there be rich and poor. Here again the *True Briton* expresses the orthodox point of view. In a serial dealing with a miners' strike, the day-to-day sufferings of these workers are recognized, but justified.

> It is evidently a part of the social and moral economy of the world, that extremes should meet. It is the lot of one portion of our fellow-creatures to pass their lives in labouring for living or for wealth— not in sight of the warm sun of heaven . . . but in glimmering darkness, in subterranean caverns, in strange and murky mines . . . where danger and death stalk round in fearful proximity. And yet, how could the world be carried on, but for the product of these labours? The misery and danger of thousands of our fellow-beings, is the source of happiness to millions.[2]

Similarly, Marryat in his more consistent moments claimed that

> the luxury, the pampered state, the idleness—if you please, the wickedness of the rich, all contribute to the support, the comfort, and employment of the poor. You may behold extravagance, it is a

---

[1] *True Briton*, ii (1852), 3, and i (N.S. [1852-3]), 200.   [2] Ibid. i (N.S.), 883.

,vice; but that very extravagance circulates money, and the vice of one contributes to the happiness of many.[1]

But, perhaps because it is a little more complex, this defence of the *status quo* is not often expressed in fiction.

Another argument was that inequality gave a stimulus to effort, being

> a wise provision, not permitted in order to make the lowly creep, and cringe, and sacrifice their very souls to please the princes of the earth; nor yet designed to authorise men to strut and stalk about as if they were the elect of Fortune; but to serve as a stimulus to the exertions of the lowly,—an incentive to the high to adorn and maintain that elevated spot whereon Fate has placed them.[2]

Others maintained that the hostility felt by the poor towards the rich was based on a mistaken theory of happiness. Since joy and sorrow are evenly distributed among men, the rich are no happier than the poor. This belief was expressed in a very striking way by a writer in *Ainsworth's Magazine* for 1854, who in an article describing the lot of the agricultural labourer writes, 'He *can* expect nothing but the filling a pauper's grave,' and two pages further on says:

> 'God be thanked that the very humble agricultural labourer, who is so ignorant, so excluded from the bright intellectual world, who, in a sense, it must be confessed, is of such trifling value in creation, can yet delight in existence, and be thankful for its gift.'

We find this attitude in fiction, as in Mrs. Grey's novel, *The Little Wife:*

> Oh! if we could bear in mind, that elevation in life is no security against the severer ills of the world, but rather, in most cases, a fearful increase of their bitterness, we might save ourselves and others, from many unnecessary strivings and disappointments!

(The main characters in this story are Lord and Lady Elmsdale, who end up in a state of ideal happiness, while the only prominent character who belongs to the middle class makes a considerable fortune, and weds the daughter of an earl in the last chapter.)

---

[1] *Mr. Midshipman Easy*, 1836, iii, 223.
[2] Mrs. Thomson, *Widows and Widowers*, Parlour Library, n.d. p. 309.

This view of the equal distribution of happiness among all ranks could be very well combined with the belief that the inequality of men was decreed by God, and the two ideas together must have been a great comfort to people who had mild qualms about living conditions among agricultural labourers in Dorset or mill-hands in Liverpool. The conjunction is expressed in a passage from Carleton's story *The Clarionet*, a story which describes the lives of a very poor man and woman with pathos and tenderness.

> Whilst the great look down upon the lowly as the heirs of wretchedness and misery, and find upon examination that those whom they despise are happier than themselves, this—if anything can—ought to teach them that humility which proceeds from a sense of God's goodness in equalizing the enjoyment of all ranks and conditions.

Finally, it was often stated or implied that the poverty of a large section of the poor was their own fault. The more religious periodicals, like the *True Briton*, the *Home Friend*, and *Cassell's Illustrated Family Paper*, upheld the duties of early rising, unremitting industry, honesty, frugality, civility and cleanliness, and attacked the poor for being lazy, spendthrift and intemperate. Many stories show the former qualities as leading to prosperity, the latter to disaster. This attitude is part of another of the interesting paradoxes in the general attitude to class distinction. It has already been shown that, while the rich are often attacked, most writers aim at leaving their favoured characters respectable and comfortably off, and often push them along up the social scale. There is a similar contradiction in the attitude to the poor. As well as the virtues enumerated above, contentment with their position is frequently put forward as a cardinal virtue among the humble. Yet almost all their other virtues are such as will help them to rise in the world, and are often shown as doing so. Through the period under discussion, there is a steady increase in the number of stories about the careers of self-made men. Just why anyone who was contented with his lot should want to rise is never made clear. It was not submission to his superiors that lay behind a typical *Family Herald* success story called *The Reward of Perseverance*, in which occurs the following passage:

> Faint murmurs of approbation are heard, even from the courtly throng there assembled, as Sir George Murray leads his lovely wife up to the throne and presents her to the sovereign. Public services of great value to the country had won him a baronetcy.

Sir George, who started life as the son of a small farmer, later attended 'a large dinner-party, given by the Earl of S——'. Here he made a speech which clearly conflicts with the teaching of contentment to the poor. It ends:

> 'When I recall the time that I was a cabin-boy, buffeted and kicked as any one or every one pleased, and contrast it with the present moment, which finds me a guest at the table of one of the noblest men of the realm, I may surely be pardoned for a little exultation. If the details of my life should induce only one of my countrymen to pursue a similar arduous path, I shall rejoice in the opportunity which has been afforded me of relating them.' [1]

The solution of the puzzle may lie in the fact that any threat to the established order of society was felt to come, not from men who became wealthy by their own efforts and quickly assimilated themselves to the rank for which their particular degree of wealth fitted them, but from the great majority of the poor who had no hope of improving their condition. It was for their ears that the sermons on content were preached, and to them were addressed the references to the folly of strikes, into which simple creatures were led by paid agitators. And it was for them to remember that

> by far the greater part of these very rich men had either raised themselves, or their fathers had raised themselves and their families, by frugality, economy, hard work, foresight, providence, right-mindedness, and a proper employment of their talents, joined to rigid self-denial—denial, that is, of what we commonly call the enjoyments of life—to be capitalists. [2]

While certain fairly well marked attitudes towards the rich and the great can be observed in this fiction, the middle classes are

[1] *Family Herald*, xiii (May 12, 1855), 26.
[2] *True Briton*, ii (N.S., September 1, 1853), 61.

seldom made the object of either praise or blame. There are occasional references to the peculiar virtue of middle-class heroines, who are more modest and less mercenary than girls of a higher rank. And there is frequent mention of the vice of emulating the manners and habits of the aristocracy. 'The middle class of English society, which is always trying to push itself a step up the mighty ladder, whose height is both dizzy and dangerous', is a description from a novel by Mrs. S. C. Hall, who probably knew what she was taking about. A particular object of amusement is the evening party which aspires to a tone out of all accord with the social position of the characters, like the one given by Blanchard Jerrold's Mrs. de Gospitch, which Viscount Humbug so unaccountably failed to attend.[1] Another is described in *Widows and Widowers:*

> Comfortable and happy vulgarity! genius of true enjoyment! wherefore didst thou on this occasion veil thy face, and place the phantom of gentility before those who would gladly have forgotten that such a spirit existed?

It is good to know that in this case 'the purgatory to which gentility had condemned the party' did not last, and they all settled down to honest enjoyment before long. Women are accused of this fault rather than men, and there are many short stories attacking the wife who eggs her husband into unwise expenditure in emulation of the neighbours, or of people of a higher social class.

But apart from these points, the typical qualities of the middle class are displayed in this fiction, but are not a subject for it. It is very likely that those who know most about these qualities will see in many of the general attitudes we have been discussing evidence that the writers reflected the middle-class point of view, in the attitudes to female virtue, for example, to the education of women, and to the primary importance of love in marriage. The same may be true of the supremacy of conscience and the homage paid to religion, the generally depreciatory attitude to foreigners, the conservative attitude to class distinction, and the belief in the

[1] In *The Disgrace to the Family.*

inevitability with which virtue is rewarded by riches and social position. But these attitudes are not consciously identified as belonging to a particular class. They are not objects to be discussed in this literature, but assumptions that underlie it.

The poor, however, like the aristocracy, are a frequent object of discussion (though many writers ignore their existence as completely as did Jane Austen). Our knowledge of the truly dreadful lives they so often endured at this date, and our familiarity with the compassionate treatment they receive from writers like Dickens, do not prepare us for the ruthless realism of certain references to them. When Ellen, the heroine of *Discipline*, begins as a reformed character to take an interest in the poor, she is disappointed to find them 'selfish, proud and sensual, as well as cunning and improvident'. *A Warning to Wives*, describing a group of poor seamstresses, speaks of 'their vain, silly, envious jabber . . . their low intrigues, their vile confidences, their petty calumnies, and their atrocious lies'. Mrs. Marsh in *Angela* stigmatizes

> those ill-regulated passions, those low and sordid views, those coarse manners, and that gross language, which disfigure that ill-educated and half-civilised portion of mankind which still, alas! makes up so large a portion of every society—and which it has been, perhaps, too much the habit of mistaken philanthropists in fiction lately to disregard in their manner of writing to and about them.

She comes down strongly in favour of the new Poor Law, and attacks those who teach the poor to cast the responsibility for their lot on their superiors, instead of blaming their own vice, intemperance and sloth. She insists that 'the Englishman (and woman) of the lower classes does not require what is commonly called pleasure'. And Reynolds, in theory the champion of the poor, describes them as vicious and depraved, omitting any reference even to what was generally admitted to be characteristic of them, the way in which they helped one another.

In contrast with this rigorous attitude—which is found in the novels rather than the periodicals—the poor are at times represented as the patient and innocent victims of circumstances or of individuals. Novels about Ireland do this pretty consistently, and the same note is struck by Mrs. S. C. Hall (an Irishwoman) in *Marian*. Speaking of some poor people, she says:

> *They starve* together—a luxury which our modern Lycurguses deem it not right their subjects should enjoy in the new slave-state of Old England. Our poor now, the greater number of whom have contributed to the support of the state, starve in loveless solitude!

More acute but no less pitiful are the words put into the mouth of a character in the *Home Friend* of 1854, who defends the poor against charges of improvidence in the following words:

> 'I have scarcely the heart to wish them different. Their raven-like dependence on Providence which distinguishes them is a part of their happiness. If they were to share our solicitude for the future; our anxious care, as concerns our family, for the days to come, the load that now lies comparatively easy upon them, would utterly crush them, and make life intolerable.'

It is a great pity when this sort of attitude is accompanied by the most ridiculous and unreal idealization of the characters, as when peasant girls are given some of the more absurd qualities of fine ladies. Mave and Sarah in *The Black Prophet* have small hands and beautiful taper fingers, with which all their lives they have done the work of Irish peasant girls. When Pennie, in one of Griffin's *Tales of the Munster Festivals*, has to be told that her lover is cleared of a charge of murder, 'although the mode of her life and education exempted her in general from the danger which might be apprehended in such cases to a person of more refined habits or a more nervous constitution', yet there were grave apprehensions about the possible effect of the shock. (As 'her senses failed her, and she fell on the floor in a strong convulsion fit' when she heard the news, it is dreadful to think how a more delicate organization would have responded.)

The best stories about the poor are written by people who see them as individuals rather than as a class, who neither attack nor defend them, who look on them as human beings to be understood and pitied like any others. But such stories are few. Mrs. Gaskell's contributions to *Household Words* are the outstanding example. The courage, uprightness, tenacity and loyal devotion, the miserliness and asperity of the people in the north of England are described with tenderness and respect—for their own sake. The important thing about a story like *Lizzie Leigh* is not the poverty of the characters, but their qualities, their relations with one another, and the compassion which embraces the outraged harshness of Lizzie's father, and the pharisaism of her brother, as well as her own sufferings, the humble patient love of her mother, and the divine charity of Susan. Carleton in *The Clarionet* comes near to the same kind of beauty; the story of the blind musician and his wife is unmarred by the melodramatic incidents that creep into some of his other novels, and is told as an idyll of the humblest, tenderest love. Unfortunately his style, though sometimes as pure and clear as Mrs. Gaskell's, is often turgid and artificial, thus spoiling the simplicity of the tale, a fault very common in this kind of literature. But he sees the poor in this story as individuals, to be loved or hated for their own sake, not as members of a certain class, to be judged by its relations with other classes.

Servants, as a species of the poor, tend also to be either idealized or depreciated as a class. *Susan Hopley*, by Mrs. Crowe, really has for its theme the sentiment, 'there are few friends more valuable than an attached and worthy servant', while in *Marmaduke Wyvil* we find a similar lament:

> Those were the days when servants waited on their masters not with lip-loyalty alone, but with heart service; when the dependant was not looked upon as a mere hireling . . . nor the employer regarded solely as the dispenser of food and raiment, to be cheated as much, and obeyed as little as practicable; which, I fear, will be found the case too often, despite the much-vaunted superiority and intelligence of these modern times.

Most individual servants in this fiction are presented as carelessly conceived examples of a stock type, the old family retainer; like the old manservant in *Trevelyan*, who sobs aloud at his mistress's funeral, or like Bessy, in a serial called *The Autobiography of an Heiress*, who, when the family fortunes are restored, and she is asked whether she wishes to leave them and carry out her own plans, replies, 'For twelve years, madam, since the day I left my father's house, I have had no plans.' The author comments on 'the simple grandeur of this reply'.[1]

There is also the type of the comic servant, like Lover's *Handy Andy*. But it is the rarest thing for servants to be made the main characters in a story, or for them to be considered except as appendages of their employers. This is part of the deep underlying conviction that only the lives of middle- or upper-class people are to be considered as the raw material of literature. For nothing is clearer than the fact that very few of our authors consider the lives of the poor to be suitable material for fiction. Just as children and old people exist for them only as they influence or are influenced by the central characters, the active and the nubile, so for the most part the poor are subordinated to the rich. They are oppressed or relieved by them, they serve them or are served by them; but stories in which they are the most important characters are comparatively few. Poor readers wanted to read about lives completely different from their own, and the most successful and widely circulated penny periodicals gave them what they wanted. Readers from the middle and upper classes did not want to read about the poor either—hence the character of novels in the Parlour and Railway Libraries, which were mostly reprints of expensive three-volume works. The unspoken implication is that prosperity and a certain social position are necessary to make life interesting and happy.

This seems the best place in which to consider the attitudes to work and money revealed in this fiction. Not that either of these topics is dealt with directly more than once or twice (as in stories like Carleton's *Fardarougha the Miser*, a good study of the conflict between avarice and family affection). But a very interesting diversity of viewpoint is revealed, particularly about work. On the one hand is the belief that work is a necessary evil. This view is consistently reflected in the novels, and of course in much periodical fiction too. The lucky man is he who is born with

[1] *Cassell's Illustrated Family Paper*, v (N.S., March 24, 1860), 267.

enough money to free him from work—he is the gentleman. He who is not born to wealth may do one or other of three things. He may marry money, scratch along as best he can with what he has, or else make up his mind to work just long enough to enable him to retire on the proceeds, and begin to live like a gentleman. The first course was deprecated; the second was the one commonly adopted. Seldom in the novels does the hero have recourse to the desperate expedient of making money for himself.

It has already been pointed out that your true hero was a man of birth and property. When young, he might spend his days amid the frivolities of fashionable society; as he grew older, he became preoccupied with affairs of state or with the management of his property. Novelists like Mrs. Gore, Mrs. Trollope, Mrs. Marsh and Lady Charlotte Bury never suggest that their heroes are unhappy, even when their whole time seems to be spent on trivialities. They never think of them as needing settled gainful occupation to make life worth living, any more than Jane Austen expected Charles Bingley or Henry Tilney to work six days a week. Nor do they expect such of their heroes as are poor to take any active steps to improve their condition. In *The Ward*, for example, Mrs. Trollope depicts Sir Charles Temple and Major Heathcote as estimable characters. Sir Charles, inheritor of an enormous country house and a small income, divides his time between visiting his widowed mother in Florence, and coming home to shoot and to cultivate the society of his old neighbour, Mr. Thorpe. He leads a perfectly blameless and useless life. (There is not even much suggestion that he takes an interest in agriculture.) He is, and his existence is its own justification. Major Heathcote and his wife and eleven children must subsist on his half-pay and very little else. The Major is sensible, magnanimous and kind, but there is no hint that he makes or should make any effort to augment his income, though his wife sits at her sewing all day, and must scrape and save to keep the family alive. The creators of Pelham and Cecil, again, never envisage them as carving out their own fortunes. (The contrast in this respect between Pelham and Peisistratus Caxton is instructive.) A man

Lord Saxondale, an impostor.

waits till he is offered a living or a secretaryship or a sinecure, or till a convenient relative dies and leaves him a fortune. Even Mrs. Crowe, otherwise so clear-sighted, is full of pity for a man who has fretted his life away in litigation over the property of his deceased wife. She never hints in *Lilly Dawson* that the better course for Colonel Adams would have been to forget his doubtful title to the estate of his first wife, and set to work by his own exertions to provide a more congenial standard of living for her successor. And in *The Ladder of Gold*, the man who knows he is too poor ever to be accepted by a rich man as suitor to his daughter quite explicitly rejects the suggestion that he should settle down and work, in the hope of making himself more eligible.

'What is there for me?' he cries. 'To select a profession, for which I have no inclination or capacity: work hard against the grain of my feelings—grind my heart to powder—and, perhaps, get nothing by it in the end—neither fame nor profit.'

The author does not condemn the attitude which sees in work a horror far greater than the certainty of losing the woman he loves.

A corollary of this was the readiness of wives and mothers and daughters to scrimp and save for the sake of their menfolk. This was fair enough when the money went towards education or other worthy objects, but a modern reader is staggered by the calm assumption that when a male member of the family gets into financial difficulties through gambling or other folly, the females should cheerfully economize to pay his debts. In Hook's *Cousin Geoffry* not only do Mr. St. Aubyn's wife and daughters suffer great hardship through his passion for play and his son's, but it is clear that Mrs. St. Aubyn would be less than the perfect wife she is if she remonstrated with her husband. Woman's part is to console, to endure, to patch up the trouble—not to stimulate, or if necessary goad her son or husband into exertions which would lead to more financial and emotional security all round.

When gentlefolk are compelled to work, they suffer. Mrs. Marsh in *Angela* describes their situation as follows: 'Hard labour, which sends the frame accustomed to it to enjoy the elysium of unbroken slumber . . . leaves *them* oppressed with toil—faint, fevered with unusual exertion, weary, exhausted, nervous.' The limits of safety are reached in a story in *Eliza Cook's Journal* about a family in which the mother and five daughters, the youngest of whom is fifteen, are represented as doing all the work of a household which includes, in addition to themselves, the father and two brothers, one of whom is under fifteen. One sister, we are told, often looked weary, but the others bore up pretty well. The author makes a cautious comment:

> I do not think that hard work would have done the same for the sisters in a town; but in combination with the purity of the air, and the quiet and regular manner of their life, it had been beneficial to the sounder constitutions among them.

And it must be realized that this writer is advocating something revolutionary, that middle class people in financial difficulties should dispense with domestic servants. The novelists never go so far.

The periodicals, however, often express a different point of view. The *Family Herald* in 1843 has a story in which work appears as a villainous necessity, but one which the hero accepts because he wishes to protect his mother and sister against 'the rough usages of an unkind world'. He goes abroad to make his fortune, and marries (for love) an Indian heiress. That is the end of work for him.

> The amount of property George had received with his bride was amply sufficient to relieve him from the necessity of going to sea again professionally; and he now gave himself up wholly to the company of his wife and relations, with whom he lived in the closest bonds of harmony, and amply repaid the maternal love that had been lavished on his infancy.

This is already one step from the attitude of most novelists. George does not care for work, regarding it as a disagreeable burden to be cast off at the earliest possible moment. The life of a gentleman is his ideal. But all the same he is prepared to face up to his obligations and take active steps to discharge them.

Still further removed from the novels is the attitude shown in a little tale from the same volume called *The Benefits of Industry*. It describes a hard-working Persian who gets great pleasure from growing flowers for sale. 'They were *his* flowers; *he* planted them, *he* watered them, pruned and nurtured them.' When for a while he tired and a genie did the work for him, he soon realized how much happier he was in doing it himself. Here we get a glimpse of a new attitude, which regards work as more pleasurable than idleness.

This new point of view, which is characteristic of the periodicals rather than the novels, sees work as a duty, a pleasure, and a blessing. 'Religion and morality, as well as physical law require work as a duty', says a writer in the *Leisure Hour* of 1860. ' To work is honourable in either sex, whilst idleness is a reproach.' The story of a rich man who has become poor, and been reduced to honest toil and to help from his children, ends with the youngest saying: 'We were none of us happy when we were rich and did not work. So, father, please do not be a rich man any more.' [1] And a woman who has behaved foolishly and become estranged from her husband is advised to find her salvation in work:

> It is only by daily work of mind or hands, in which service or benefit to others is involved, that perfection of character can be attained; and this work she must engage in from a sense of duty, from a consciousness that she is walking in a right path, and with a determination to view that apparent friend as an enemy who would interfere or turn her from the work she has been sent into the world to perform. [2]

We have become very familiar with the idea that work, which for most of us is equated with earning a living or caring for a home, is one of the great objects of existence and the alleviation of its miseries. Thus we fail to see that this idea conflicts with a much older tradition, which held that the good life implied freedom from this kind of work, the disengagement of energy, and its devotion to better objects than earning a living. A man might have to devote part of his life to getting rich, but only as a means to an end, like the one who, having made a fortune by the time he was in his early thirties, 'shook the dust of commerce

[1] *Cassell's Illustrated Family Paper*, ii (March 10, 1855), 75.
[2] *Ladies' Treasury*, v (1861), 176.

from his feet' and went abroad in search of culture, and in the hope of becoming a man of the world. Such ends frequently involved much activity, as a man undertook the cares of government, of scholarship, of administering his own estates. But these things were not gainful work. This tradition was reflected in much nineteenth-century literature. But so was the idealization of work, especially in fiction directed to an audience for whom work was an inescapable and life-long necessity. Occasionally it goes even further than pointing out the blessings of industry, and hints at a compulsion with which we are familiar today, and which has many curious implications. So a man who at the age of forty receives a large legacy does not do as his wife wishes, and retire, for 'he dreaded the idea of an inactive life'. But this inability to enjoy leisure is seldom apparent.[1]

Whether a man worked for it or not, money was assumed to be a good thing, not essential for happiness, but desirable for all that it could do, especially for others. So a girl who hears of a huge legacy probably awaiting her and her sister says,

> 'Not that I care for wealth . . . for its own sake, or, as far as I am personally concerned, for the comforts it procures, but that I pine to restore mamma to peace and ease, to be free from this terrible struggle for daily bread, this incessant pondering upon the worth and value of money. And as much as all, to be able once more to indulge in the luxury of helping others.'[2]

Except for the clause 'as far as I am personally concerned', I suppose that most of us would regard this as a sensible attitude.

But there are several respects in which the attitude to money reflected in this fiction is alien to our ideas. One is the extraordinary omnipresence of debt. Poor people become indebted for

---

[1] Trollope in *The Three Clerks*, ascribing to avarice the intense laboriousness of so many men, yet finds it inexplicable. For, as he truly says, 'Men are not now more keen after the pleasures which wealth can buy than were their forefathers. One would rather say that they are less so. The rich labour now, and work with an assiduity that often puts to shame the sweat in which the poor man earns his bread' (*The Three Clerks*, 1858, ii, 310). The motives underlying the extreme industriousness of so many Victorians, in fact even more than in fiction, are much more complex than Trollope suggests.

[2] *Cassell's Illustrated Family Paper*, ii (March 10, 1855), 75.

food and rent, rich people for the same things on a more magnificent scale; youths at university, young men about town, great business men, fine ladies, poor washerwomen—all are entangled in the traps set for them by landlords, tradespeople, Jews, milliners, professional moneylenders, 'tallymen' (who sold finery to working-class women on a time-payment system), and so on. Those who are inclined to look back with nostalgia on the mid-nineteenth century as a period of great commercial expansion and prosperity may gain some consolation if they realize that in fiction (and in fact) the financial position of individuals was often alarmingly insecure. Not only are many people represented as able to live solely by running into debt, but members of the middle and upper classes accept their perilous situation with a nonchalance which is staggering to the twentieth century reader, haunted by the spectre of his overdraft. Their insecurity did not cost them many sleepless nights—there was always the continent to escape to. Least of all did it drive them to work, in order to improve their position. Something would turn up. Their attitude is the subject of a very interesting passage in *The Confessions of an Etonian*. This story claims that it was practically impossible for a boy at Eton in the early nineteenth century to escape being in debt right throughout his schooldays. The system of credit in the school shops and various other things are blamed for this. Describing the typical Eton boy, the writer says:

> Thus he was never out of debt; indebtment became a habit; gradually it assumed the character of one of the conditions of his existence; and at last he grew resigned to the evil as one of the ills of life, which boys as well as men are heir to.

Which is an excellent statement of the attitude revealed in this fiction. Debt was like a congenital physical or mental infirmity. To struggle against it was a sign of virtue, but to be overcome by it was hardly a matter for blame.

A second way in which we cannot share the attitude to money reflected in this fiction is in the belief, most apparent in evangelical periodicals, that piety pays dividends. The (converted) man who does the will of the Lord is bound to end up with a good bank balance, like the characters in the stories in the *Sunday at Home*. One such was a blacksmith who worked well, but alienated his neighbours by his religious beliefs and practices. He thus became poor, but he stood firm till fortune changed and he became much more prosperous than ever. The title of this story tells its own tale—it is *Nothing Lost by Serving God*. Belief in God implies belief in the rewards of His service, but few of us would maintain or wish that those rewards should be material ones. Neither of course did most Christians a hundred years ago, but those who did have left their mark on fiction, both what was ephemeral and what was destined to endure.

A third and almost universal element in the attitude to money was a belief in the virtues of thrift, especially among the lower orders. The implications of this, and of the change that has since taken place, are so far-reaching that they cannot even be touched on here. It seems curious, however, since thrift was so generally extolled, that indebtedness should not have been more generally reprobated. But in part it may have been a matter of class. Debt as a generally accepted condition of existence with which people came to terms pretty easily was more the prerogative of the upper and middle classes. Workers, who must, unless they were thrifty, eventually become a charge on the rest of the community, were required to save, and in many cases were eager to do so, if only to protect themselves from the bogey of want.

About money most writers were fundamentally agreed. It is in their attitudes to class and to work that we find a diversity of opinion that is still reflected in modern literature. Distinctions of class and wealth are still very great in popular fiction and often greatly resented; and though the hero and heroine nowadays both work, work is frequently regarded as a necessary and tiresome preliminary to a better state of life—whether the holiday at the sea or a retirement spent in a passionate devotion to horticulture.

XIV

RELIGION AND MORALS

IN reading this fiction, one is struck by its generally religious tone. Innumerable references, some of them very brief and slight, others more substantial, make it clear that the existence of God is taken for granted. Almost always it is clear that the conception of God is definitely Christian, though not necessarily Christian in the most orthodox sense. The characters who are meant to attract the reader's sympathy are usually represented as pious, at any rate in the sense of showing deference to the deity. Heroines in particular have recourse to prayer, and there is a good deal of rolling of eyes to heaven in a more or less prayerful way. Sorrows and joys are commonly regarded as sent from on high, moral laws are given a religious foundation, and moral decisions are based on religious considerations.

But one is equally struck by the fact that specific references to Christianity as represented by the different sects and their ministers are as often as not extremely hostile. It is very important to remember that the Parlour and Railway Libraries do not at this period include what are commonly called 'religious novels'— religious in the sense in which the word could be applied to the works of Charlotte M. Yonge, or, on another level, to those of the Rev. W. Gresley,[1] novels that definitely support the teaching of a particular sect. Many of the novels published between 1847 and 1860 in these series show the strong and sincere faith of their authors, but they are not concerned with advancing any specific system of beliefs. The same, if we except the evangelical publications, is true of the cheap weekly and monthly periodicals. While

---

[1] This writer expounded Tractarian principles in novels like *Charles Lover; or, The Man of the Nineteenth Century* (1841), and *Bernard Leslie* (1843). Doctrine was sandwiched between slices of story, in which all the good characters were church people, all the bad ones dissenters, liberals, democrats, socialists, believers in the ballot, etc. The books were published very cheaply.

both novels and periodicals show an imprecise but universal deference to Christianity in general, they support no particular sect, allude only to the most generally accepted doctrines, and very often contain characters or passages which show hostility to a definite sect or its adherents.

Recognition of this hostility to one or other religious sect and to sectarianism in general is crucial for understanding the general attitude to religion in this literature. The established church is let off the most lightly. Reference has already been made to the fashionable parson in the *Mysteries of London* whose amorous activities finally ended with his committing murder and suicide. But this is an isolated instance, and nobody would dream of taking Reynolds very seriously in a matter where his prejudices were so aroused. The Rev. Reginald Tracy is not one of a class of fornicating, murderous and suicidal Church-of-England clergymen. Indeed, there are many examples of virtuous parsons, like the old curate in *Alice*, and Mr. Leslie in *The Young Prima Donna*.[1] On the other hand, there are equally numerous references to coldness, laziness, snobbery and apathy in the Anglican clergy, and it is pretty clear that our writers had no compunction in making their charges. Tractarianism not unnaturally came in for an occasional hit, as in the account of the Puseyite parson in *The Gold-Worshippers*,[2] and in the portrait of a young man in *Singleton Fontenoy*,[3] who 'puzzled himself with the doctrines of a very clever set at Oriel, who first made him a proselyte, and then a laughing stock'. It was also, quite naturally, attacked in the evangelical periodicals, but that was on doctrinal grounds, and has little use as evidence of a general attitude.

Nothing, however, was said against the commonly accepted doctrine of the Church of England. The same is true of the often tasteless and unpleasant attacks on Roman Catholicism that occur in the periodicals, especially during the earlier part of our period. Of course the full force of these was disguised by the fact that they occur in historical stories, like Reynolds's *Mysteries of the Inquisition* and *Wagner: the Wehr-Wolf*, and to some extent carry

---

[1] By Mrs. Grey.   [2] By Emma Robinson.   [3] By James Hannay.

on a tradition established in the Gothic novel. All the same, few Roman Catholics could have enjoyed reading a Salisbury Square story like *Giralda; or, The Invisible Husband*, which showed a villainous friar acting as pander to the Duke of Aragon; or one like *Gertrude; or, The Queen's Vengeance*, a long serial in the *Family Herald*, set in the days of Queen Mary, and describing King Philip and another villainous cleric as thirsting for the embraces of the virtuous and Protestant heroine. In one episode, the hero, who has been imprisoned by the monk, turns the tables on him by tying him up and gagging him with his crucifix and beads, a specially pleasant touch. In the novels we find an occasional though more gentlemanly attack, as in Marryat's picture of the Irish priest in *Peter Simple*, cadging, casuistical, foolish and mean. G. P. R. James is hostile to Roman Catholicism, as when in *The Forgery* the hero scouts the possibility that he might have been converted by the Italians and Spaniards among whom he spent his youth. 'I took the Bible and common sense,' he says, 'and I could not be a Papist.' On the other hand, a good many historical novels (and an occasional serial in the periodicals) give a favourable picture of the old religion, novels like *Whitefriars* by Emma Robinson, *Jane Seton* and *Bothwell* by James Grant, and *The Hour and the Man* by Harriet Martineau. Michael Banim's *Father Connell* gives a lively and charming portrait of an Irish priest. Even *Reynolds's Miscellany* in its later and more regenerate days gives, in a serial called *The Lady of Castle-Rose*, an attractive picture of a French convent.

Then there was a fierce attack on the extreme evangelicals, and particularly on the figure of the dissenting or Low Church parson. This was no doubt more because of the humorous possibilities of these figures than through opposition to their teachings. We are all familiar with the attitude adopted by Dickens in *Pickwick Papers*, but probably less aware of the fact that Mr. Stiggins and 'the shepherd' were members of a fairly numerous literary class. One such member, the Rev. James Cartwright in *The Vicar of Wrexhill*, was probably created quite independently of the more famous character, for *The Vicar of Wrexhill* was first published in

1837. Already in Mr. Stiggins and Mr. Cartwright appears the emphasis on certain qualities as typical of the worst type of dissenting or Low Church parson—his power over women (and their power over him, which stimulates him to a kind of oily lasciviousness), his fondness for creature comforts, his rapacity, his smooth tongue, his lack of any true religious feeling, and his skill in disguising his lust, gluttony and avarice beneath a mask of hypocrisy. Some, if not all, of these qualities are attributed to a number of characters, like Parson Hartley and the other evangelical toadies who surround Mrs. Maurice in *The Lottery of Marriage*, and the sycophantic chaplain in *Tracey*,[1] who was given a parish as an inducement to him to influence his step-daughter in favour of the unprincipled and profligate hero. Mr. Pratt, frequently referred to as a 'heavenly spirited man', took a typical view of his parochial duties. These were 'chiefly of a visitorial character; he consoled the widow, and cheered the solitude of the spinster; men he shunned, but the tender and helpless sex were dear to this "sweet saint".' Meanwhile he grew rosy and sleek on his generous stipend.

Reynolds in the *Mysteries of London* depicts the 'shepherd' at his lowest, in the person of a man who takes to religion as a relief from pecuniary embarrassments, and seduces a young woman in response to a 'vision'; Arthur Robins in *Miriam May* gives the most detailed account in the picture of the Hon. and Rev. Calvin Slie, who neglects his pastoral duties, especially to the poor, enjoys the best food and drink, suns himself in female admiration, writes tracts, preaches against 'the machinations of Rome', and prays in public at every opportunity, however unsuitable.

While some of these attacks on particular sects (for example, that made by Robins, and possibly Mrs. Trollope's too), were animated by the writer's zeal for a different party, this does not generally seem to be the case. Periodicals like the *Family Herald* and the *London Journal* at one level, and like *Chambers' Journal* and *Household Words* at another, were more or less specifically opposed to sectarianism of any kind, and the same is true of many

[1] By Mrs. Thomson.

novelists. The editorials of the *Family Herald* in particular preach a vaguely impressive religion which is not even certainly to be identified as Christianity, and clearly not with any particular branch of the church. A story in *Household Words*, telling of the life of a spinster in a quiet country town, describes the preacher she hears on Sunday as follows: 'There is not a word of controversy in his sermon. It is very simple; all about kindness, and charity, and tender-heartedness, and the pleasant duty of loving one another.' [1] In *The Gold-Worshippers*, alongside the unfavourable pictures of the Puseyite clergyman and the sour old lady of obtrusively evangelical opinions, we find the following description of the heroine:

> And what was Charity's religion? She would have been puzzled to describe it in the formula of any catechism. She was a christian in heart and soul, and it is therefore probable that she was unfitted to be of any sect in particular.

In *Marian*, Mrs. S. C. Hall refers to 'one of those narrow-minded fanatics who steep God's love and mercy in their own bitterness, and then proclaim it to the world under the title of religion', while one of the heroines of *Martin Beck* [2] is impressed by the catholic nature of the books in her fiancé's room. 'A Christian!' thought Katharine, 'no more, and no less.' And Mrs. Crowe's heroine in *Lilly Dawson* is described as having 'an internal consciousness of God, and an innocent piety, little perplexed by creeds or dogmas'.

These attacks on particular sects and on sectarianism of any kind, are, except for the teaching of the definitely religious periodicals, characteristic of the attitude to religion taken up by most popular fiction at this date. And they are not to be confused with atheism, agnosticism, indifference, or even with theism. When, in *The Vicar of Wrexhill*, Henrietta Cartwright rejects the curate's suit with the words 'I AM AN ATHEIST,' the unaffected horror of the lively Rosalind represents what would have been the general reaction of characters in these stories to such a statement. When a story in *Chambers' Journal* for 1855, describing

---

[1] *Household Words*, xi (June 16, 1855), 473.   [2] By A. Harris.

Sunday in the Australian goldfields, says, 'The melancholy truth is, the digger is the child of today, and religion concerns him little'; or when one of Reynolds's heroines describes the power of prayer in the following words: 'I believe that there is something consolatory, soothing, and encouraging in prayer: and even if this be only the work of the imagination, the effect is still the same', in both cases we feel a shock, not at the nature of the sentiments, but at their utter incongruity with the explicit and the implicit assumptions general in this literature. Equally uncharacteristic is the vague theism of editorials in the *Family Herald*, and of Reynolds's more respectable characters in the *Mysteries of London* (whose theism is probably introduced simply as an indication of their respectability). Popular literature at this period was definitely on the side of Christianity; it frequently took for granted the existing organization of the established church, but apart from that it seldom gave its support to any particular religious body. References to church-going are surprisingly few and unemphatic. One feels that neither the publishers of the genuinely popular cheap weeklies nor those of the Parlour and Railway Libraries were at this date prepared to assist the circulation of sectarian literature.

Yet we receive the impression that much more than lip-service is being paid to religion. In the novels of writers like Lady Charlotte Bury, Mrs. Marsh, Mrs. Hall, Mrs. Oliphant, Lady Scott, the Banims, Carleton, James Grant—indeed, in most of the novels in these series, and in most periodical fiction too—there is a vein of personal, non-institutional piety. Characters make and carry out moral decisions in accordance with orthodox Christian belief, and writers comment on them from the same point of view. To give some examples, Mrs. Oliphant, especially in *Margaret Maitland*, sees all things referred to one standard. Life is the pathway to death, and all our thoughts and actions are to be considered *sub specie aeternitatis*. This notion of life as a probation for eternity is often found, and suffering is to be regarded as necessary for perfecting the soul and fitting it for heaven. So Mrs. Marsh says of Flavia in *The Wilmingtons* that she was in every way fortunately situated: 'There were but few things wanting: difficulty, which calls forth energy; contradiction, which exercises temper; sorrow, which exalts faith; death, which teaches truth.' Adversity is the nurse of more than worldly virtue. Mrs. Yorick Smythies in *A Warning to Wives* goes so far as to blame one of her characters, a loving wife and mother, for returning to the normal social life of her class after her little boy has been seriously ill. Ada has nursed the child with the greatest care and devotion, but is blamed for not having learned her lesson. 'No, no, Sorrow has not yet fully chastened her spirit; she determines to celebrate her child's recovery by a splendid ball; and Vanity and Mammon claim her once again.' While in *The Little Wife* both Mrs. Grey and her heroine see the loss of one of the latter's children as a warning against idolatry.

The attitude to suffering is crucial for understanding one important thing about religious and moral attitudes in this fiction. Most novelists, and many writers in periodicals too, accept it as an inevitable and indeed a blessed part of life. This attitude must be understood in contrast to their comparative indifference to what might be called 'collective' suffering, as caused by things like bad working conditions, bad housing and sanitation, inadequate wages, and all the other wrongs that were arousing so much attention among reformers. Reference was made in the last chapter to the theory that human suffering is pretty evenly distributed, and that the poor and the rich share it equally, which theory was sometimes used to justify the continued existence of bitter poverty. Now, while the conclusion is intolerable, and even the theory in such a simplified form is very dubious (for the quality of human suffering can hardly be disregarded, and a calculus of suffering is as impossible as a calculus of pleasure), yet human life is full of sorrows, and certain *kinds* of suffering must be endured with little hope of amelioration. No amount of social reform is going to protect us against painful experiences arising, for example, from inequality between our powers and our ambition, from failure to measure up to our own ideals or those of the society in which we live, from disappointing and being disappointed by the people we love; above all, nothing is going to protect us against death. This is where the religious and moral attitudes embodied in this fiction come out very strong. It is all very well to laugh at death-bed scenes in Victorian literature, and very funny they can be too, but non-essentials should not blind us to the fact that the actors in these scenes faced death with courage and resignation. Underlying their fortitude was faith in an after-life, one of the fundamental and generally accepted doctrines of Christianity. Whether the writers themselves, or their readers, entirely believed this doctrine, who is to say? The point here is that they understood its power as a foundation for the good life, and held it up as an ideal.

There is implied an enormous contrast between this attitude to life, ancient, traditional, fundamentally other-worldly, and that which is found more commonly in the periodicals than in the novels, the attitude which stresses instead the demands of this world and the progress that is being made in meeting them. The contrast can be illustrated by two quotations. In one, the Irish novelist Gerald Griffin gives his view of things. This is a world 'where *no* positive happiness can exist—but where life runs on between regret for the past—want for the present—and hope for the future'.[1] (The contrast with the next world is clearly implied.) In the other, a character from a success story in *Household Words* sees mankind

> 'all advancing, some faster, some slower, to a better education, a better social condition, a better conception of the principles of art and commerce, and a clearer recognition of their rights and their duties, and a more cheering faith in the upward tendency of humanity.' [2]

On another level, the contest between the claims of heaven and earth is pointed by a statement made by the gossiping inquisitive neighbour of a pious old lady. The neighbour finds the old lady's religious habits intolerable, and expresses her feelings: 'Of course . . . we all must die, that everybody knows without a clergyman

[1] *Tales of the Munster Festivals*, 1848, p. 140.
[2] *Household Words*, i (August 10, 1850), 475. The story is by William Howitt.

to come and tell one; but I cannot see any use in holding one's
nose over it, as one may say.' [1]

The belief in progress is generally dissociated in our minds from
Christianity, with its emphasis upon the claims and values of
another world. But in this fiction the cleavage is not apparent.
Reynolds, perhaps the only writer of whom one could say from
the study of his works alone that he was probably not a Christian,
deals rather with detailed descriptions of present evils and vague
threats of revolutions than with efforts at the improvement of the
existing state of affairs. There is nothing in the attitude of those
who express the views of orthodox optimism to indicate a
cleavage between it and orthodox religion. Indeed, in a book like
Sir Philip Hetherington we find explicit both a firm and uncom-
promising Christianity, and also a firm belief that 'we do live in
wonderful times, and more wonderful ones are coming on'.
Sometimes religion itself is seen as partaking of the general improvement of all things, as in the following passage: 'The world
is getting better: men, women, and children, the land itself,
religion, commerce, politics, are all together getting better.' [2]
The divorce between orthodox Christian thought and a belief in
progress is never suggested in this fiction.

It is the fashion at present to turn up our noses at the nineteenth-
century belief in progress, equally with the nineteenth-century
emphasis on death. Yet the improvement in social conditions with
which the belief in progress was so closely connected, both as
cause and as effect, was perfectly real. Men were learning that
some—indeed much—suffering could be averted by hard work
and good will. If from this they were led to a rather ill-defined
belief that *all* suffering could ultimately be avoided and heaven be
built on earth, it was no groundless or utterly foolish delusion
that they cherished. In the same way, the belief that suffering is an
inevitable part of human experience, that 'neither men nor
women are good for any thing who have not been well broken
up by suffering', [3] is certainly respectable. Many people still hold

[1] *Trevelyan*, 1860, p. 252.   [3] *Eliza Cook's Journal,* xi (Sept. 30, 1854), 353.
[2] G. E. Jewsbury, *The Half Sisters,* 1848, ii, 52.

it, however much they dislike the conclusion that was often drawn from it, the conclusion that there was no great call for large-scale attempts to reduce avoidable suffering as much as possible. We cannot simply laugh at the two views of life presented in this fiction, as we can, for example, laugh at its view of women. There is much in them of enduring truth.

Whichever view was assumed by a writer to be valid, there was no paltering with the obligations it imposed. Whether life was seen as offering great rewards in this world, or as the pathway to a better, the individual's part in it was clearly defined; at whatever cost, he must do his duty. He was master of his own destiny. He had the moral law within him, expressing itself through his conscience. Let him heed its voice, struggling if necessary with unregenerate impulses, and victory was certain. It was generally assumed that it lies within ourselves to make of ourselves what we will; hence, if we fail, the undying pangs of remorse. No excuses for wrongdoing are seriously entertained. We have the power to do right, if we care to exert it. The formation of our characters is our own responsibility, and we are equally responsible for our influence over other people.

To this extreme and healthy voluntarism, so much in contrast with the modern attitude of rueful acceptance of our own follies and weaknesses (whatever we think of other people's), is due in part the moral rigour, the atmosphere of strenuous conscientiousness, which permeates this fiction. Men's duties were clearly defined by laws based on religion; in fact, as was suggested in the chapters on the relations between men and women and between parents and children, they are made unnaturally clear, since the possibility of a true conflict of duties is seldom seriously faced. That was the first element in creating the feeling of moral stringency. And the second was the belief in the final and complete responsibility of the individual for recognizing and doing his duty. The villain in Lady Lyons's *Olivia* expresses a modern point of view when he asks,

'What are we to do—*we* who are sent into this world with strong passions and vivid capability of enjoying life and its various pleasures?

We do not make ourselves; and as it is not our fault if nature makes us prone to err, I am also convinced we cannot change our dispositions.'

To this is opposed the consistent view of the author and of almost all her contemporaries. 'We have all of us counteracting qualities, physical as well as mental, sufficient to enable us to struggle with our natural weaknesses whatever they may be', she says. And 'there *are* antidotes *in* ourselves *to* ourselves.' Of the weak and erring father she says: 'Let no one therefore suppose that we are the mere creatures of circumstances. St. Lawrence's actions were in his own power.'

We can control ourselves and master our own feelings and desires if we want to. Heroines, and even heroes, may pine and die as a result of the violence of the struggle, but they have the victory. Pretty clearly implied is something of the doctrine of original sin, which makes the struggle universal and permanent, for 'in the purest and the highest hearts, there is—there ever will be—one small drop of selfishness much to be guarded against'.[1] Thus the fight against our weaknesses is a part of human destiny, closely connected as a rule with our vulnerability to suffering; and like the latter it is morally beneficial. As the *Home Friend* says of one of its characters, 'the smooth part of life had always been hers, and little experience is requisite to prove that few under similar circumstances have become either bright ornaments to society or striking examples of Christian attainments'.[2] Moreover, the struggle invariably led to happiness, whether of the more ordinary kind, arising when obstacles were overcome, fortune changed, and the long and patient fight was rewarded; or else the less obvious and more rarified kind, the chastened happiness that comes from the consciousness of having done right. Thus, in *The Only Daughter*,[3] the unloved Ruth lived for others. She was content

> so long as it remained for her to suffer alone and occasionally to forget her sorrow, in the delicious thrill of self-approval, and the soothing consciousness of the success of her great efforts, and the boundless happiness which she was securing for those whose happiness was dearer to her than her own.

[1] G. P. R. James, *The Black Eagle*, 1859, p. 291.
[2] *Home Friend*, iv (N.S., March 1856), 206.   [3] By Harriette Campbell.

Even more important in this fiction than 'the delicious thrill of self-approval' were the undying pangs of remorse. These are well described by one stricken creature:

> 'There is no peace for the wicked, Félicie!—no peace for the wretch ever haunted by a remembrance grievous and intolerable—a fearful vision which I have often called on death itself to hide from me—a retrospection that time obscures not, darkness conceals not, sunshine lightens not—a phantom that never vanishes, changing its form a hundred times a day.' [1]

No character with whom author or reader was in sympathy was allowed to forget the past. Sometimes remorse was eventually fatal, as in *The Forgery*, where it killed both the supposed and the actual father of the hero, the former for making Henry the scapegoat for his sins, the latter for not acknowledging his son. At other times it merely poisoned existence, as in *The Flitch of Bacon*, where Sir Walter expiates by half a lifetime of misery his unjust suspicions of his wife, which had led to a duel and to the death of an innocent man. And sometimes it haunts people who have really been compelled to a wrong action, like the gipsy woman in *Castle Avon*,[2] who was driven to murder in order to protect the infant foundling Claribert. It is difficult to see how else she could have achieved her object, for the child's life was at stake, yet she is eternally unhappy as a result. This is completely in accordance with the general moral attitude of this literature. Duty is duty, quite easily discernible and quite within our powers of performance. If we do right, we shall in one way or other be rewarded—if we do wrong, we shall suffer for it here and hereafter.[3]

[1] Mrs. Grey, *Sybil Lennard* [1854], p. 265.   [2] By Mrs. Marsh.

[3] The contemporary attack on the morality of *Eugene Aram* was justified by the standards of the day (and by modern standards too) better than the reviewers realized. Eugene Aram is presented as a person with whom we are to sympathize, but he is affected by regret for his great crime, and not remorse. In his confession he describes his 'chiefest penance' as 'the humbling part of crime, its low calculations, its poor defence, its paltry trickery, its mean hypocrisy'. Not the consciousness of wrong doing but its inconvenience afflicts him. In connection with the crime of murder, such an attitude is shocking. It is also very unusual in the fiction of the mid-nineteenth century. Hardened criminals are of course familiar figures in this literature, but either their crime is of a kind to which popular sentiment had long offered a sort of pardon, like that of the highwayman, or else the reader is not expected to sympathize with them.

There is one instance of the universal homage paid to duty which is particularly relevant to the theme of this book. That is the frequency with which writers of fiction at all levels anticipate and defend themselves against possible charges of moral laxity, and proclaim that their object is always to elevate and reform. Fiction was still at this period a little on the defensive, and writers of cheap fiction were specially anxious to establish their claim to respectability. The official manifestos of new periodicals frequently defend this claim, but quite often it is stated directly in the stories themselves. Reynolds justifies his description of 'the shoals, the quicksands, and the rocks of vice' by saying that a knowledge of them is necessary for those who would follow virtue. The preface to *Recollections of a Detective Police-Officer* [1] assures the reader that in the book he will find nothing 'to in the slightest degree aliment a "Jack Sheppard" vocation, nor one line that can raise a blush on the most sensitive cheek'. Marryat in *Midshipman Easy* declares that he has chosen 'this light and trifling species of writing, as it is by many denominated, as a channel through which we may convey wholesome advice in a palatable shape'. At the conclusion of an immensely long serial in *Lloyd's Penny Weekly Miscellany* the writer claims that he has done as the novelist should ever do—remembering that he 'wields an instrument powerful for good or evil', he has tried 'to elevate virtue and nobleness—to show how the pure, the truthful, and the innocent achieve, even in their sufferings, a higher triumph than can ever be produced amid the turbulence of vice'. [2] Innumerable stories end with a pious hope that the experiences of the characters may bring warning or inspiration to the reader, in which case the writer will not have written in vain. For the same well defined and firmly conscientious motives as direct the actors in the stories are supposed to direct the writers of them too.

This supremacy of conscience, this atmosphere of strenuous moral endeavour, is probably the most impressive quality of this fiction. Both the content and the validity of the moral law were

---

[1] By 'Waters' (W. Russell).
[2] *Lloyd's Penny Weekly Miscellany*, iii [1844], 384.

generally recognized. Authors and characters alike were confident that they knew where they were going—to heaven, or to a better earth—and just how they should behave to the other pilgrims on the way. There were differences of opinion on a few points, but none that threatened their splendid unanimity on matters like the central doctrines of Christianity, the authority of husbands and fathers, the true nature of man, and still more, of woman, and the fundamental wisdom of class distinction. Some understanding of this unanimity is the reward that a study of this fiction offers the modern reader. It would be foolish to pretend that much of it is worth reading even once for its own sake. Masterpieces are seldom long forgotten. But it reveals to us that world, distorted, idealized, yet recognizable as their own, which ordinary people a hundred years ago wanted to read about; from its assumptions about life, death and immortality we may learn a little more about their deepest convictions.

XV

CONCLUSION: A QUESTION OF TASTE

BUT, it may be objected, what about the literary problem from which this study of early popular literature began? What about comparative levels of taste at different periods of history? For this, after all, is to many people the most interesting issue of such an enquiry as that on which this book is based. Something has no doubt been learned about popular literature a hundred years ago, but how does it compare with its counterpart today?

Here, however, arises exactly the same difficulty as led to the writing of this book. For if one obstacle to the rational discussion of changing levels of taste has always been very general ignorance of the popular literature of the past, an even greater obstacle is ignorance of the popular literature of the present. The reader may now have some faint idea of the sheer volume of such literature a hundred years ago. But what is it in comparison with the literal tons of comics, pulp magazines, women's magazines of all kinds and prices, men's magazines, picture papers, pocket novels and so on, which now cater for an enormously increased public, a public which has on the whole much more time for reading than that of the past? Successful business men though they were, William Chambers and Edward Lloyd were pigmies compared with the individuals and organizations which are now engaged in producing literature for the people. Who will combine the monumental patience with the synoptic vision essential for seeing a wood among so many trees? What oracle can we look for, to tell us how in fact the reading of the half-educated in the mid-twentieth century compares with the reading of the still less educated a hundred years ago?

A few modern writers, it is true, have taken the trouble to study in detail some branch of modern popular fiction, and we have books like Wertham's *Seduction of the Innocent*, on American

173

comics, and articles like George Orwell's excellent 'Raffles and Miss Blandish'. But that he should acquire a comprehensive know-ledge of modern popular literature seems too much to demand of any intelligent person—and the unintelligent cannot help us. Nor is there any real help in vague impressions gained by glancing at the comics or true confession stories confiscated in the classroom, at the magazines in the dentist's or hairdresser's waiting-room, at the paper-backed novel which has been left behind by the previous tenant of the holiday cottage. Each of us who prides himself on his modest powers of discrimination has in this kind of way gained some impression of some sorts of modern popular literature, and very violent our feelings about it tend to be. But such judgments are strongly emotional, and if we are honest we must admit that they are inadequate as the basis of a reasoned comparison between modern popular literature and that of the past.

And, in any case, is this comparison possible? Is this question of comparative levels of taste perhaps unanswerable? Apart even from the consideration that pushpin may after all be as good as poetry, and one book as another provided it gives pleasure, can critical methods and language developed in the study of great literature be applied to literature written only to entertain the reader without making him exert himself, and to make money for the writer? And can we justify the general tendency to let moral judgments influence our evaluation of popular literature in a way and to an extent that we avoid in criticizing more serious writing? Are we right in assuming, as I think most of us do, that extremes of horror, violence and vice are tolerable subject matter for the serious writer, whose attitudes we can respect even if we do not share them; so that in judging his work we can forget the ethical problems that arise when such matters are described by the writer whose motives and attitudes we do not trust? Again, to consider a more practical difficulty, is cheapness as a criterion of popularity in fiction of much importance today, as compared with a hundred years ago? And how far is popular fiction now influenced by the other so-called 'mass media'—cinema, radio and television—so that in fighting for its public it must try to outdo the stimulation they provide?

A hundred years ago the writer of cheap fiction had things much more his own way, for even the flourishing popular theatre provided a very limited amount of competition.[1] Should we connect the almost incredible development of the use of illustrations over the last hundred years with the fact that popular literature has come to provide for a less and less literate public? To read even a penny dreadful it was necessary to be fully literate, in the mechanical sense of the word, but much modern fiction can in some sense be understood by those who can hardly read at all. The tastes of such a public must have some effect on what is being provided for them. These and many other problems at once obtrude themselves when we think of going beyond the fairly simple matter of describing the popular literature of a restricted period. And they are problems this book cannot solve.

But while I lack the knowledge of modern popular literature which is needed for their solution, and have no intention at this stage of embarking on a discussion of critical principles, it would not be fair to conclude without a positive statement of opinion, however hedged about with reservations, however consciously based on undiscussed assumptions, however uncertain and incomplete it may be. Is there, in fact, any good reason for the view so forcibly advanced by Mrs. Leavis in *Fiction and the Reading Public*, and so widely held since, that popular literature and popular taste have deteriorated greatly during the last hundred years? It is important for the reader to understand that in so far as this view depends on Mrs. Leavis's own account of the situation a hundred years ago it is ill-supported. This account is based on the records of their reading left by a few very exceptional working-class men

[1] The popular theatre at this period is a subject well worth investigation. Articles in *Household Words* for March 30 and April 13, 1850, and May 22, 1858, give entertaining descriptions of plays shown at theatres on the south bank. The first two of the articles are by Dickens himself. A similar description is given by Albert Smith in *The Scattergood Family*. The plays are very similar in plot and event to penny dreadfuls, and indeed an examination of the titles in such series as *Dick's Standard Plays* and *Lacy's Acting Edition* shows that some penny dreadfuls were apparently presented in dramatized versions.

who had a passion for self-improvement, and on a cursory examination of one or two cheap periodicals. An obscure little journal, the *Family Economist*, is cited as the 1848 equivalent of the modern monthly for the home, though contemporary discussions of popular literature never mention it, and though the *Family Herald* and the *London Journal* were then flourishing, and a few years later had between them a circulation of three-quarters of a million. Reynolds and his pretentious manifestos concerning his desire to elevate and educate the industrious classes are taken at their face value, but the simultaneous appearance of his *Mysteries of London*, generally accepted at the time as the most widely read of all novels then appearing in penny parts, is ignored. So is the earlier existence of chap-books, 'bluebooks', tracts, almanacs, last dying confessions and accounts of executions, love songs, etc., not to mention the mass of indecent literature to which Mayhew and others refer. The horrible degradation of the lower classes at this period, the dreadful conditions under which they lived and worked, are so little understood that the writer believes that 'the journeymen and peasants and tradesmen of the first half of the nineteenth century did not go to books for an escape from their lives but to qualify themselves to live to more purpose'.[1] And so little is known of their reading that she can say that 'the popular Press about 1850, then, has the dignity of the best papers of the age'.[2]

But in spite of the fact that the evidence for the conclusion is poor, the conclusion may still be right. I think that in 1957 (it is less clear about 1932) the indications are that a good deal of popular literature is inferior to that of the past. It is true that the general standard of the fiction reprinted in the Penguin series, for example, is much higher than that of the Parlour and Railway Libraries. Much modern fiction which could never be called popular is now available at a very low price. And now, as a hundred years ago, popular fiction includes a great many books which harmlessly meet the perennial human demand for effortless entertainment. Compare Mrs. Trollope with Mrs. Thirkell,

[1] Q. D. Leavis, *Fiction and the Reading Public*, 1932, p. 206.   [2] Ibid. p. 177.

G. P. R. James with Georgette Heyer, Mayne Reid with Agatha Christie, and there seems little difference in merit. Such writers will always have a useful function to perform. But a huge number of very different novels are now published, in both England and America. (In discussing modern popular fiction it is almost impossible to discriminate between what is English and what is American in origin; a great deal of what appears in British countries is certainly of American origin.) And at the lower end of the scale come novels which are very bad, much worse than the feeblest romances by such a writer as Mrs. Grey, who wrote *The Young Husband* and *The Little Wife*, or the most sensational of the penny dreadfuls. The same is true in the case of periodicals, as is shown by comparing the *Family Herald* of the mid-nineteenth century with many modern magazines for women and girls. Some of these latter contain at times stories which attain a certain standard of literary sophistication. But others, mostly American in origin, such as those of the true confession kind, are very much worse than their older counterparts, while a glance at the illustrations of Wertham's *Seduction of the Innocent* will show that, however insistent Lloyd may have been on larger eyes and more blood in the illustrations of the first penny dreadfuls, neither he, nor even Reynolds in his earlier days, entertained the idea of exploiting, for a largely adult public, situations which are now depicted for the eyes of children.

It would therefore seem that in the case of both novels and periodicals there has at the lower end of the scale of merit been marked deterioration of standard over the past hundred years. This is the crucial point. Standards do not seem to have changed much at the top of the scale; popular literature of the better kind, whether cheap or not, seems to appeal by the same means and to the same kind of reader at both periods (largely by not asking us to make any intellectual or imaginative effort as we read). But there is no evidence to suggest that bookstalls a hundred years ago were displaying and selling bad literature of the kind that is seen today. Certainly there can have been no comparable impression of senseless violence, irredeemable folly and sheer vulgarity, such as is now created by displays of the poorer paper-backed novels, by many comics, and by many magazines.[1]

But this opinion is based on moral rather than on literary grounds. It is doubtful whether, with respect to structure, characterization or style, there is much to choose between popular fiction at different times. The same weaknesses are found, the same stereotyped plots; the same stock situations and characters; at the lowest level the uncertain grammar, at a higher level pretentious writing full of ornate phraseology, inaccurate use of the less common words, and ridiculous metaphor; at best, a totally undistinguished style.[2] In both cases the reader is confronted with limited, erroneouor is nsensitive ideas about life and people and their problems.

But in much of the poorest and most widely disseminated modern fiction these ideas seem to show a change, and it is this change which I believe finally to justify the opinion that popular fiction today is worse than that of a hundred years ago. I shall very briefly consider two instances of such changed ideas, chosen because they seem the most important, but certainly not the only ones to be found. The first is the attitude to female virtue. One of the rare examples of a new form of popular fiction is the modern 'true confession' story, the heroine and narrator of which is inevitably a faulty character. For she tells the story, and she must have something to confess. She is untruthful or unchaste, unjustifiably rebellious against authority and often involved in actual crime. But she is found now in all kinds of romantic fiction, not just in stories that use the confession technique. It is true that

[1] Richard Hoggart, in *The Uses of Literacy*, Chatto and Windus, 1957, discusses modern popular fiction, and in particular sex-and-violence novels, in considerable detail. He makes interesting and useful comparisons with similar fiction in the earlier twentieth century.

[2] Examples of similarities in plot and characterization would be too tedious, but as far as concerns style the reader should compare the examples of errors made in penny dreadfuls, described in Chapter II, with the following, all typical expressions taken from a few recent books, magazines or comics: 'You're mother called me'; 'Please don't feel obligated to me'; 'You were different than I expected'; 'Lay still till he gets here'; 'The last hour swept on sylvan wings'; 'Just a second that kiss lasted, but it was like a row of cannon invading my lips'; 'Her hair was a pale brown ocean that swirled with motion and threw off the sunlight that bounced into it.' The idioms differ, but the mistakes are of the same kind.

the stories usually show her learning by bitter experience that virtue is more likely than vice to lead to a comfortable and prosperous existence. But before her reformation she is—she must be—depicted as an attractive figure, with whom the reader is intended to identify herself. The heroine's rebellion against authority, her love affairs, her criminal and near criminal activities are excitingly and sympathetically described, while the standards and ideals to which she ultimately conforms are extremely vague, and when defined are second-rate. A sort of 'decency' is the usual ideal, while American stories of this type often end with the 'fresh start' of a second marriage after the first has ended in divorce.

While a stock situation of romantic fiction has always been the interruption by adverse circumstances of the early happiness of a pair of lovers, in the past the interruption has been due most commonly to the folly and vices of outsiders, sometimes to those of the hero, least commonly to those of the heroine. Even when it was the heroine's mistakes which led to her sufferings, as in some of the penny dreadfuls, the mistakes were not due to an excess of sexual passion, or to any other serious moral failing. Therefore we have here one important respect in which much modern popular literature differs from that of the past. It may still be argued that the change is not necessarily for the worse, that it is to be found in fiction at all levels, and is part of the refusal to idealize which is characteristic of the best modern novelists. But its importance must be granted. The traditional stereotype, now being discarded, of the kind, gentle and chaste heroine has had great significance in western society. Whether we like it or not, the ancient attitude to the value of chastity in women, and in general the belief that women are morally better than men, are fundamental to our culture. For a very long time women have maintained, and have been expected to maintain standards of conduct higher than those of men. (Not merely in the matter of sexual behaviour, of course.) Even if we put aside the question whether this is a reasonable expectation, and avoid the difficult problem of how far if at all our behaviour is influenced by what we read, the fact remains that the implications

of such a change of attitude in popular fiction are generally
unrecognized and may well be far-reaching. My own opinion is
that they are also disturbing. Unprepared though I am to accept
as an ideal the concept of womanhood found in early-Victorian
fiction, I yet believe that the idealization of women has had a very
beneficial effect on our society. Since I also believe that what we
read has some influence on what we become, it seems to me a
bad thing that modern popular fiction, designed as it is for an
unreflecting and uncritical public, is promulgating a lower ideal
of womanhood than similar literature has done in the past.[1]

The second way in which modern popular literature seems to
me to show deterioration is perhaps still more serious. This is in
its treatment of violence. During all my reading of the popular
fiction of the last century I did not get the same impression of silly
stupid violence as is conveyed by the illustrations and text even
of a few of the war and crime comics which are imported into
New Zealand. Yet New Zealand exercises a pretty strict censorship over this kind of literature. A much worse impression, one
of violence as more deliberate and more deliberately delineated,
is given by some of the numerous comics which are excluded
from this country. And exactly the same sort of thing is to be
found in magazines and novels. Passages such as the following,

[1] *Time* (March 25, 1957) in an article entitled 'Tin from Sin' refers to a magazine
story in which 'a teenager in 7,000 action-packed words recounts her father's
suicide, her poverty-ridden childhood with a lunatic grandmother, rape by a
giggling maniac, seduction by her boss's stepson, addiction to "sex-pills",
confinement in a home for delinquent girls ... Unlike soap opera, the average
confession story runs a gamy gamut of misadventure and misfortune whose
Boccaccian detail is tempered only by the bowdlerized prose of Hollywood.
A bastard is a "sin child" or "living proof", adultery is "cheating". But in the end
every Wedding-Ring Dodger and Faithless Mate, however devious, rises above
the blighted past.'
But the *New Zealand Listener* (April 18, 1957) suggests that the wicked heroine
is beginning to appear even in soap opera. The heroines of two serials cited are
'both unpleasant young women ... But the serials are conceived from their
points of view, and they are obviously the ones the listener is supposed to
identify herself with ... Their technique is mental torture; and this, it seems, is
respectable enough to get by the auditioners ... No doubt in a few years' time
they will come to a sticky end or be made into reformed characters; but meanwhile a grand time is had by all. And I am wowser enough to think it ought
not to be.'

taken from novels by Mickey Spillane (whose sales are said by Geoffrey Wagner in *Parade of Pleasure* to number twenty million in America alone), are quite without parallel in my reading of penny dreadfuls and similar nineteenth-century literature. They make the descriptions of cruelty in Reynolds's early works seem very tame; yet many modern stories contain the same kind of thing. The narrator in both passages is the 'good' character, as opposed to the criminals in the story:

'The little guy stared too long. He should have been watching my face. I snapped the side of the rod across his jaw and laid the flesh open to the bone. He dropped the sap and staggered into the big boy with a scream starting to come up out of his throat only to get it cut off in the middle as I pounded his teeth back into his mouth with the end of the barrel. The big guy tried to shove him out of the way. He got so mad he came right at me with his head down and I took my own damn time about kicking him in the face. He smashed into the door and lay there bubbling. So I kicked him again and he stopped bubbling. I pulled the knucks off his hand then went over and picked up the sap. The punk was vomiting on the floor, trying to claw his way under the sink. For laughs I gave him a taste of his own sap on the back of his hand and felt the bones go into splinters. He wasn't going to be using any tools for a long time.'

For laughs, indeed.

The victim of the next assault has been described as having 'a middle-aged, sensitive Latin face'. After this man has given the hero certain information, the hero blames him for the deaths of victims of the Mafia. He answers:

' "I know them! From Europe I know them and who am I to speak against them. You do not understand what they do to people. You. . . ." My knuckles cracked across his jaw so hard he went back over the arm of a chair and spilled in a heap on the floor. He lay there with his eyes wide open, and the spit dribbling out of his open mouth started to turn pink. He was the bug caught in the web trying to hide from the spider and he backed into the hornet's nest.'[1]

Now the victim here is a petty criminal, in no way responsible, except by keeping silence, for what has happened. As the hero truly says, the Italian is the helpless little man trapped between

[1] The first of these extracts is from *The Big Kill*, the second from *Kiss Me Deadly*, both published by Arthur Barker, Ltd.

two superior forces. And the hero continues, as in the first extract, to beat him up after his original purpose is fulfilled, just for the hell of it.

These examples are intended to complement the impression of the modern heroine given above, and to show the kind of hero with whom the male reader of some extremely popular modern fiction is invited to identify himself. This is not at all the sort of thing that was being discussed when, a hundred years ago, people like Charles Knight and Hepworth Dixon complained of the degraded brutality of penny dreadfuls and similar publications. In fact, a term like 'degraded brutality' as applied to fiction now means something quite different from what it meant then. Only in the writings of Reynolds, and in them only for a short time, is there any sign of violence being described for its own sake. Even then, the descriptions are comparatively restrained, and, most important of all, the violence is never the act of the hero. Moreover, the pressure of public opinion soon forced Reynolds to change his tune.

Here then, as in the presentation of the heroine, we find that the worst of modern popular literature is very different from that of the past. Most people will agree that the difference is significant. My own opinion is also that it is exceedingly sinister.

These very briefly are some of the reasons why I believe that standards in modern popular fiction have deteriorated very seriously during the past hundred years. They are moral rather than literary. The argument depends on the belief that literature influences what we are, and that the influence is most powerful when the reader is intellectually unsophisticated. Those who reject this belief may be right. For my part, I am inclined to agree with Miss Fanny Mayne, who in the *Englishwoman's Magazine* for 1852 wrote: 'When, in a tale of fiction, the affections of the reader are all drawn out towards persons of grossly immoral character, and their sympathies enlisted on their side rather than on that of those of an opposite stamp—who, by the bye, are ordinarily represented as extremely unamiable and stupid,—the story has done *its work;* and that work is a leaven of unmitigated evil.'

CHEAP PERIODICALS OF THE MID-NINETEENTH CENTURY

The British Workman (1855-1921)
Cassell's Illustrated Family Paper (1853-1866; continued as *Cassell's Magazine* 1867-1932)
Chambers' Edinburgh Journal (1832-1956)
The Churchman's Monthly Penny Magazine (1846-1867)
Cleave's Penny Gazette of Variety and Amusement (1837-1844)
Eliza Cook's Journal (1849-1854)
Englishwoman's Domestic Magazine (1852-1877)
The Family Economist (1848-1860)
The Family Friend (1849-1921)
The Family Herald (1843-1939)
The Family Paper (1856-1863)
The Family Treasury of Sunday Reading (1859-1879; continued as the *Christian Monthly and Family Treasury,* 1880-1882)
The Farthing Journal (1840)
Halfpenny Magazine (1840-1841)
The Home Circle (1849-1854)
The Home Companion (1852-1856)
The Home Friend (1852-1856)
The Home Magazine (1856-1866)
Household Words (1850-1859)
Leigh Hunt's London Journal (1834-1835)
The Leisure Hour (1852-1905)
The Literature of Working Men (1850-1851)
Lloyd's Monthly Volume of Amusing and Instructive Literature (1845-1847)
Lloyd's Penny Sunday Times and People's Police Gazette, Companion to (1841-1847)
Lloyd's Penny Weekly Miscellany (1843-1846)
Lloyd's Weekly Miscellany (1850-1851)
The London Journal (1845-1912)
The London Pioneer (1846-1848)
The Maids', Wives', and Widows' Magazine (1832-1833)
The Mother's Friend (1848-1895)
The Parlor Magazine of the Literature of All Nations (1851)
The Penny Magazine (1832-1845)
The Penny Post (1851-1896)
The Penny Story Teller (1832-1841)

The People's Periodical and Family Library (1846-1847)
The Reasoner: and 'Herald of Progress' (1846-1872)
Reynolds's Miscellany (1846-1869)
The Saturday Magazine (1832-1844)
The Servants' Magazine; or, Female Domestics' Instructor (1838-1869)
The Sunday at Home (1854-1940)
The True Briton (1851-1854)

Complete lists of the novels published in the Parlour and Railway Libraries up till 1860 are to be found in the *English Catalogue of Books, 1835-1863.*

INDEX